IT'S UP TO YOU, ABE LINCOLN

LEILA AND TOM HIRSCHFELD

ILLUSTRATIONS BY LISA WEBER

CROWN BOOKS FOR YOUNG READERS
NEW YORK

All rights reserved. Published in the United States by Crown Books for
Young Readers, an imprint of Random House Children's Books,
a division of Penguin Random House LLC, New York.

Crown and the colophon are registered trademarks of
Penguin Random House LLC.

Visit us on the Web! rhcbooks.com

Educators and librarians, for a variety of teaching tools, visit us at
RHTeachersLibrarians.com

Library of Congress Cataloging-in-Publication Data
Names: Hirschfeld, Leila, author. | Hirschfeld, Tom, author. |
Weber, Lisa K., illustrator.
Title: It's up to you, Abe Lincoln / Leila and Tom Hirschfeld ;
illustrations by Lisa Weber.
Description: First edition. | New York : Crown Books for Young Readers, 2018.
Identifiers: LCCN 2018006933 | ISBN 978-0-553-50953-3 (hardcover) |
ISBN 978-0-553-50954-0 (glb) | ISBN 978-0-553-50955-7 (ebook)
Subjects: LCSH: Lincoln, Abraham, 1809–1865—Juvenile literature. |
Presidents—United States—Biography—Juvenile literature. | United
States—History—Civil War, 1861–1865—Juvenile literature. | United
States—Politics and government—1861–1865—Juvenile literature.
Classification: LCC E457.905 .H57 2018 | DDC 973.7092 [B]—dc23

The text of this book is set in 11-point William.
Interior design by Neil Swaab

Printed in the United States of America
10 9 8 7 6 5 4 3 2 1
First Edition

*For Julie Hirschfeld: wondrous wife, magical mom,
and editor extraordinaire*

CONTENTS

A Face Only a
NATION
Could Love?

ABRAHAM, THAT FACE OF YOURS! "Awful ugly," the poet Walt Whitman called it—and he was a fan. Your law partner described your "lantern jaws and large mouth and solid nose," your "sunken eyes," your "wrinkled and retreating forehead cut off by a mass of tousled hair"—and he was one of your best friends. Your *enemies* said you looked

> Hi! I'm Walt Whitman and better-looking than Abraham Lincoln—but that's not saying much!

WALT WHITMAN

like an ape, or worse. Your wife's family thought she was crazy to be marrying you.

But look where that face of yours has landed. On billions of pennies (first president ever on a US coin). On millions of five-dollar bills. On a gigantic, majestic marble monument in Washington, DC. Even supersized on Mount Rushmore.

Who would have expected it? For as long as voting has existed, appearance has mattered in politics. Successful candidates tend to be relatively good-looking; you were, um, not. Money helps in elections as well; you were born and raised poor. Winners have also generally had fine educations; you spent less than a year in school in your whole life. So how in the world, exactly, did you become president?

And not just president, but one of the all-time greats. Many historians consider you the greatest ever, or at least up there with George Washington. You accomplished incredible things for your country:

★ You rescued the planet's major democracy from life-threatening disaster and banished slavery forever from American soil, striking not one but two world-changing blows for human freedom.

★ You helped unite not only our North and South but also our East and West, pushing forward the construction of the transcontinental railroad.

★ You spurred our development by giving free land to countless pioneer families who agreed to cultivate it.

★ You spread the benefits of higher education across the nation by creating land-grant universities that continue proudly to this day.

★ You established our national currency, our Thanksgiving holiday, and our first income tax (okay, that's not your most popular milestone).

★ On top of all that, you were one of our most technology-minded presidents ever—the only one with a registered patent to his name.

> Betcha didn't know I made Thanksgiving a national holiday at the urging of magazine editor Sarah Josepha Hale. She not only convinced me to give the people pumpkin pie—she also wrote "Mary Had a Little Lamb"!

> Yum!

How could a gangly, awkward, unschooled backwoods pauper achieve such dazzling feats? You lost your mother at age nine, you had a troubled relationship with your dad, your first professional ambition was blacksmithing, you had zero experience in military combat, and the highest office you held before becoming commander in chief was in the House of Representatives—for a single, unsuccessful term.

With the odds stacked so ridiculously high against you, what could possibly have carried you all the way from log cabin to White House?

In one word, Abraham: choices.

Every day, every person in this world makes choices. Kids, teenagers, grown-ups—they all face decisions that may seem small yet can have a huge impact on them and those around them. The choices *you* made throughout your astonishing life not only shaped who you became; they also revealed who you were all along. Your decisions exhibited an exceptional mix of empathy, craftiness, honesty, humility, dedication, and, above all, vision.

Your *toughest* calls, in particular, show how a supposedly common man can have qualities that are anything but common. Those calls sure didn't please everyone: some people swore you must be racist, while other (very different) people hated you as a tyrant. Folks almost never agreed about you and your decisions—but how could they, when the problems you faced were so difficult?

Abraham, you encountered more than your share of crossroads on your amazing journey. The choices you made changed the path of your life—and the course of humanity. We're going to look at ten such crossroads, from how you dealt with your first real career failure to how you met the major challenges brought by victory in America's bloodiest war. At each crossroads, we'll explore where you were coming from, which ways you *could* have gone, and why you chose the path you did. We're going to walk in your big footsteps and discover the earthshaking times you lived in, the mind-blowing deeds you accomplished—and the extraordinary person you really were. It's not just history, Abraham: it's *your* story.

Choice I—1835

OUT OF
BUSINESS

THE CHALLENGE

YOUR STORE WENT BUST, LEAVING you with huge debts. How can you get out of this fix?

THE BACKSTORY

LATER, WHEN YOU'RE FAMOUS, YOU'LL downplay your early years of poverty, dismissing your own story as "short and simple." Really, Abraham? In fact, your home life was pretty complicated, with many moves, deaths, and deprivations that played a major role in producing the anything-but-simple person you would become.

Your dad's father, and *his* father, each lived in at least three different parts of the country. Your dad, Thomas Lincoln, followed their example, searching for new opportunities time and again as the American frontier shifted westward. Your dad tended to move once the neighborhood became too settled, so you spent your growing years more or less in the wilderness.

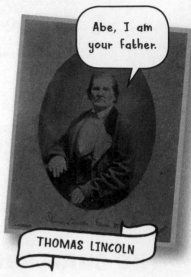

Abe, I am your Father.

THOMAS LINCOLN

Look, Dad! A new general store!

That's it! We're moving!

Your older cousin Dennis Hanks, who lived with you, will remember (when you're famous) how your dad covered you and your mom, Nancy, with a bearskin after she gave birth to you in Kentucky. As with all your family homes, your first was a log cabin built mostly by your dad.

Dennis will tell how you spent most of your boyhood wandering barefoot: "Abe was right out in the woods, about as soon's he was weaned, fishin' in the crick, settin' traps fur rabbits an' muskrats, goin' on coon-hunts with Tom an' me an' the dogs, follerin' up bees to find bee-trees, an' [plantin'] corn fur his pappy. Mighty interestin' life fur a boy, but thar was a good many chances he wouldn't live to grow up."

The brightest part of your Kentucky years was your sister, Sarah, two years older, who rocked your cradle before you could walk and, after, taught you to pick blueberries and fetch kindling. When you were six, she refused to go to her one-room schoolhouse unless "little Abe" could go with her.

(As an adult, FYI, you'll usually go by Abraham.) On the way, Sarah held your hand so you would not be scared; once there, she helped you learn your first numbers and letters. "Yessiree, Sairy an' Abe was more'n brother an' sister," Dennis will say. "[They] was best friends."

On the Move

AT AGE SEVEN, YOU MOVED to Indiana, an even wilder place—so wild that you'd one day write a poem about it:

> *When first my father settled here,*
> *'Twas then the frontier line:*
> *The panther's scream filled night with*
> *fear*
> *And bears preyed on the swine.*

You had your share of run-ins with the local wildlife, but you were never big on hunting it. Soon after arriving in Indiana, you shot a wild turkey on the wing (through a hole in the roof—nice aim for a seven-year-old!). You raced outside proudly, but he looked so beautiful lying there dead, you felt terrible. Ever after, you refused to kill any large game—a highly unusual attitude on the frontier.

You yourself almost died twice, once when you fell into a stream (luckily, a friend fished you out with a branch) and once when the family mare kicked you in the head. You were swatting her so she'd go faster but instead got yourself "apparently killed for a time."

Your folks never had much money. You spent your boyhood in ragged buckskins that you constantly outgrew, so your shinbones often stuck out beyond your pants. (In cold weather, you wore a cap of squirrel or raccoon skin.)

But the greatest lack you felt, the biggest gap in your life, was knowledge. You never got more than a few months of schooling at a time (less than a year altogether), and you never had enough *books*.

In Indiana you would tell Dennis, "The things I want to know is in books. My best friend is the man who'll git me one," but most folks couldn't help you. Few could read themselves. One neighbor would see you writing "words and sentences wherever he could. . . . He scrawled them with charcoal, he scored them in the dust, in the sand, in the snow—anywhere and everywhere."

You could even earn a few cents writing letters for folks,

DIDYA KNOW?

Abe was a huge fan of the Bard. He always enjoyed the theater and was especially fond of Shakespeare's *Macbeth*.

a reward that only increased your appetite for learning.

Over time, kind adults loaned or gave you copies of *Aesop's Fables, Robinson Crusoe,* the Bible, a biography of George Washington, and other works. According to Dennis, you were a "constant and I may say stubborn reader." You grew to love stories of all kinds: when you were reading *The Arabian Nights* to Dennis and Sarah, Dennis called it a pack of lies, to which you replied, "Mighty darned good lies."

You would memorize your favorite passages, writing them in a copybook or (if you had no paper) on boards. You also kept up with your arithmetic, scrawling these immortal lines in one math notebook that survives:

> *Abraham Lincoln*
> *his hand and pen*
> *he will be good but*
> *god knows when.*

You *were* good, at least at remembering what you learned. In your words, your mind was like some hard metal: it was "very hard to scratch anything on it and almost impossible once you get it there to rub it out." One boyhood friend will recall, "His mind soared above us. . . . He naturally assumed the leadership of the boys." An impressive feat, given that your face was never what other kids would call handsome.

When Life Hands You Lemons

WHEN YOU WERE JUST NINE, your mom died of "milk sick"; it later came out that the cows were eating snakeroot, which poisoned their milk. No one could say exactly who her father was, and she never did learn to read or write, but she was a smart, hardworking, loving woman whose influence endured in you. You cherished her as "my angel mother." Her last words to you: "I am going away from you, Abraham, and I shall not return." You helped your dad build her coffin, poor kid.

A frontier man with children needed a wife, so Thomas hauled back to Kentucky, where he had long ago proposed to Sarah Bush. After turning him down (reportedly for being too shiftless), she'd married another man and had three kids, but now she was a widow. Soon he brought them all to Indiana, where she took one look at you and your sister and gave you a good washing.

Soon enough, she managed some serious redecorating in the old cabin. A wooden floor, for starters, instead of the dirt you'd grown up with. Whitewash on the walls instead of bare planks. And, most important to her, happy children instead of sad ones.

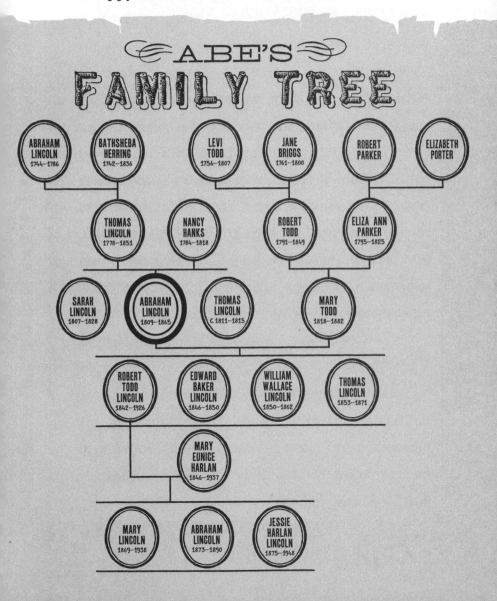

ABE'S FAMILY TREE

ABRAHAM LINCOLN 1744–1786
BATHSHEBA HERRING 1742–1836
LEVI TODD 1756–1807
JANE BRIGGS 1761–1800
ROBERT PARKER
ELIZABETH PORTER

THOMAS LINCOLN 1778–1851
NANCY HANKS 1784–1818
ROBERT TODD 1791–1849
ELIZA ANN PARKER 1795–1825

SARAH LINCOLN 1807–1828
ABRAHAM LINCOLN 1809–1865
THOMAS LINCOLN c.1811–1815
MARY TODD 1818–1882

ROBERT TODD LINCOLN 1842–1926
EDWARD BAKER LINCOLN 1846–1850
WILLIAM WALLACE LINCOLN 1850–1862
THOMAS LINCOLN 1853–1871

MARY EUNICE HARLAN 1846–1937

MARY LINCOLN 1869–1938
ABRAHAM LINCOLN 1873–1890
JESSIE HARLAN LINCOLN 1875–1948

This new mother loved you and your sister, Sarah, as if you were her own kids. You were "a boy of uncommon natural talents," she'll recall. "I never gave him a cross word in my life. He was kind to everybody and everything and always accommodated others if he could." Your frisky sense of humor endeared you to her: you were always full of jokes and tales.

Your creativity sometimes led you into mischief, as with an epic prank you played on your stepmom when you were sixteen. She was a well-pleased homemaker that Sunday, with a fresh coat of white paint inside the cabin. While she was at church, you saw a neighbor boy playing in the mud, and that gave you an idea. You picked him up and helped him walk his muddy feet up one wall, across the ceiling, and down the other side! (She was a good sport about it after the initial shock, and you were happy to repaint.)

Yet over all your boyhood pleasures loomed one enormous shadow: your dad saw little value

in learning, so you could never really please him with what you did best. He made his living with his hands, mostly in carpentering and farming, so he insisted on the same for you. You always had manual labor to do, if not for him, then for neighbors who would pay him (you might get a small share). Fields had to be plowed, crops harvested, firewood chopped, ten-foot logs split into rails for fences. You used your ax most days from age seven to twenty-two, and you used it well, but your heart was never in the work. You'd rather have been reading, reading, reading. You'd even carry a book for when the plow horse rested between rows.

Thomas wanted to see tools like these in Abe's hands—not books!

Your dad was a harsh taskmaster, perhaps because his childhood was even tougher than yours: at age six, he saw his own dad slain by an Indian near the family cabin—and might have died himself, as he cradled his dying father, if his older brother had not shot the Indian first. Unlike you, he grew up a hard man, barely literate. If he caught you with a book when you were supposed to be working, he might grab it and throw it aside. Dennis, who saw him beat you more than once—even knock you to the ground—will recall that you "never bellowed, but dropped a kind of silent, unwelcome tear."

Still, your unusual height and strength made you a valuable worker: you grew to be six foot four and could lift and carry a six-hundred-pound chicken coop.

As your strength increased, you could earn more and more for the family by doing jobs for other settlers. You were nearly nineteen, working at a neighbor's house, when you heard that your sister had died in childbirth. "I will never forget that scene," the neighbor will recall. "Abe sat down in the door of the smoke house and buried his face in his hands. The tears slowly trickled from between his bony fingers

DIDYA KNOW?

In the 1800s, men's average height was only 5'6". At 6'4", Abe would have seemed like a *giant*!

and his gaunt frame shook with sobs. We turned away."

Death had robbed you of the person who meant the most to you in life: "From that moment on, I felt very alone in the world." You accompanied your family on one more move, from Indiana to Illinois, when you were twenty-one, but a year later, in 1831, you moved away on your own. You loved your stepmom, but your dad had given you so little affection (was it because he never had a dad to show him how?), and had made your life so difficult, that you would rarely agree to see him again.

NEW SALEM, NEW START

YOU LANDED IN THE TINY Illinois settlement of New Salem, in existence for only about three years when you arrived. You were "a piece of floating driftwood," you'll recall, that happened to "accidentally lodge" there. Situated on the Sangamon River, New Salem had fewer than a hundred people, but you managed to find work with a merchant named Denton Offutt. First he hired you to build a longboat, captain it all the way down to New Orleans, sell the boat and its cargo, and bring the cash back by steamboat. (He must have trusted you.) You did such a fine job that he then hired you as an assistant in his store.

You quickly got to know the people of New Salem—including the "Clary's Grove Boys," roughnecks who often disturbed the peace. Their leader, Jack Armstrong, challenged you to a wrestling match soon after your arrival. Rather than back off, you fought him to a draw (some say you were about to win), and after that you were friends.

You also became friendly with several local farmers, who lodged you in their homes in exchange for work. You made additional contacts by joining the debating society, which met twice a month to discuss hot topics such as slavery,

FUN FACT

The bout with Jack Armstrong was not Abe's first entry into the wrestling ring. He was a skilled fighter, competing in a style more closely linked to today's hand-to-hand combat. In fact, out of more than 300 matches, historians can confirm only one instance where Abe lost.

treatment of the poor, and women's education.

The people of New Salem must have liked you, because they suggested you run for the state legislature just *eight months* after you hit town. In March 1832, you took out an ad in the county paper, introducing yourself to voters elsewhere in the district. It included this passage:

EVERY MAN IS SAID TO HAVE HIS PECULIAR AMBITION. WHETHER IT BE TRUE OR NOT, I CAN SAY FOR ONE THAT I HAVE NO OTHER SO GREAT AS THAT OF BEING TRULY ESTEEMED OF MY FELLOW MEN, BY RENDERING MYSELF WORTHY OF THEIR ESTEEM. HOW FAR I SHALL SUCCEED IN GRATIFYING THIS AMBITION, IS YET TO BE DEVELOPED.

That's for sure, Abraham. The good news is that you got 277 out of 300 votes in the New Salem area. Unfortunately, other voters in the district didn't know you yet, so you failed to win overall—that time.

Before the vote, though, you did win a different kind of election: as captain of your volunteer company in the only war in which you'd ever bear arms. It began when fighting broke out between Sauk Indians, led by Chief

Black Hawk, and Illinois settlers; soon the US Army got involved. The Black Hawk War lasted only two months, and you never saw combat (except for "a good many bloody struggles with the mosquitos").

Still, your adventure was important for several reasons:

★ It showed that people trusted you with authority. The Clary's Grove Boys all voted for you, and Jack Armstrong served as your second-in-command.

★ During the war, you met Major John T. Stuart of Springfield, a lawyer. Until then you'd thought of becoming a blacksmith, but he inspired you to study law instead.

★ You showed leadership by saving the life of a friendly Indian who came into camp bearing a pass from a US general. Some unruly volunteers wanted to shoot him, pass or no pass, but you stepped in the way. One man called that cowardly behavior, to which you retorted, "If any man thinks I am a coward, let him test it." No one stepped forward, and the Indian left safely.

Around that time, Offutt went out of business. You bought another store with William Berry, who turned out to be a terrible partner. Between his drinking and your inexperience, the place shut down within a year.

Luckily, by then you had friends who helped you get part-time work as the New Salem postmaster, which didn't pay much but did let you read all the newspapers that passed

through your office. You increased your income with work in land surveying, which was harder labor (charting property lines through miles of wilderness) but paid better and also introduced you to folks all over the county and beyond.

Your expanding network stood you in good stead when you ran again for the legislature in 1834. This time, in the words of a local observer, "Everyone knew him; and he knew everyone." A typical episode occurred when you were campaigning in the countryside, and some men harvesting in a field said they would never support a man who couldn't hold his own cutting wheat. "If that is all," you replied, "I am sure of your votes."

And with that you picked up a sickle and led them in clearing the field—winning every vote there. *That* election went to you by a wide margin. Not bad for a twenty-five-year-old with less than a year of schooling!

To make a good impression in Vandalia, the state capital at that time, you borrowed money to buy a suit. Your first session, early this year—1835—offered you priceless experience: almost all the other representatives were older, and about a quarter were lawyers. The assembly chamber was not very fancy, what with the sandboxes for tobacco spitting and the occasional chunk of plaster falling from the ceiling, but it gave you a taste for politics you would never lose. You managed to impress the Speaker enough that he appointed you to ten committees—particularly striking given that he was from the dominant Democratic Party and you were in the Whig Party minority. (Democrats in 1835 generally favor farmers and states' rights; Whigs tend to promote business, banking, the federal government, and public projects like roads and canals.)

THE CHOICE

NOW YOU ARE BACK IN New Salem, fresh from your first legislative session, but you've got a problem—a big problem. William Berry, your good-for-nothing partner, died in January. The store you and he ran is history, but it still owes money to suppliers all over the region. With Berry gone, creditors want you to pay them everything out of your savings—oh, wait, *you have no savings.* Yikes! Your life is looking kind of ruined, just when you were getting started. Can you even hope to find a way out of this mess?

WHAT DO YOU DO, ABRAHAM? SELECT ONE:

A. Skip out on your debts.

After all, that's what Denton Offutt did when the store went belly-up the first time, not uncommon behavior in the freewheeling West. And it *is* Lincoln family tradition to pick up stakes when the grass looks greener elsewhere.

B. Pay the debts, but only your half.

Berry is dead, so the whole obligation is legally yours. However, you could probably negotiate some discount with your creditors, along the lines of "Accept half or get nothing." People, in general, would rather get some money than no money. But would you risk your honorable reputation this way? Word has it that once, when you realized you had shortchanged a customer by a few pennies, you walked four miles just to hand over the proper amount. That's simply the kind of guy you are—and may be one reason you got those 277 out of 300 New Salem votes in your first campaign. Do you want to lose the good name you've built for yourself?

C. Pay the debts in full, but over time.

Because your creditors are as far away as Ohio, you can't settle most of these debts with manual labor as you've done in the past—only cash will do the trick. You would need to auction off most of your possessions just to pay the first installment, and then struggle for years to get by while you paid the rest. Are your honor and reputation worth this extreme financial hardship?

D. Marry rich and pay everyone now.

Okay, you're not exactly a ladies' man. You like females but have seldom felt at ease around those your own age. At dances in Indiana, you'd be the one surrounded by guys eager to hear your jokes—leaving the annoyed girls with a scarcity of dance partners. According to Dennis Hanks, "Abe was always mighty popular with the boys, but the girls would just as soon spit in his eye." Even if you could marry for money, though, would you want to?

THE REVEAL

Y OU CHOSE . . . C. **Pay the debts in full, but over time.** You don't skip out on your debts. Even though the practice may have been all too common in the Wild West, you aren't like most other people. And you have absolutely no interest in following in your dad's footsteps by moving from place to place to place.

You also decide not to pay only half the debt. You legally owe the whole amount, and your sense of honor forbids you to try to wiggle out of it.

So you bite the bullet and pay back every penny.

THE AFTERMATH

THE DEBT'S A HUGE SUM, so it ends up taking about eight years to pay off. You have to sell your surveying equipment and horse just to make the first installment, and it's not until 1844 (when you're thirty-five) that you feel on solid financial footing.

Your decision does carry a heavy cost in dollars and stress, but its benefits will prove far greater. Honoring the debt establishes your reputation as Honest Abe for life. You aren't doing the right thing for political gain, though; you're doing it because it's the right thing to do.

IN ABE WE TRUST.

And while you don't seek romance for financial purposes, recently you *have* been courting one woman. Her name is Ann Rutledge, her dad helped found New Salem, and you and she are going steady. Death comes to dash your happiness one more time, though, when Ann catches typhoid fever in August 1835. Her loss hits so hard that you can barely eat or sleep, confiding to a friend that you can't even "bear the idea of its raining on her grave." Her brother will recall, "The effect upon Mr. Lincoln's mind was terrible; he became plunged in despair, and many of his friends feared that reason would desert her throne."

In the 1800s, it is still shockingly common for people to die before their time, as you will (sadly and too often) be reminded.

THE MARRYING KIND?

THE CHALLENGE

YOU'VE FOUND SOMEONE TO MARRY after all. You're engaged! But if your feet were any colder, they'd be frozen solid. Should you get married, push the wedding back, or just bail out?

I'm having second thoughts.

THE BACKSTORY

IN THE STATE ASSEMBLY, YOU reconnected with your army friend John Stuart, who practiced law in Springfield and shared rooms with you in Vandalia while the legislature was in session. He helped you study law, which in those days mostly meant reading books and attending court sessions. You could often be found with a law book on your lap, studying barefoot under a hillside oak. (You haven't yet managed to find comfortable shoes for your size 14 feet, so you frequently go barefoot or in slippers.)

You began visiting Stuart's office when you could get to Springfield, the county seat, about twenty miles from New Salem. According to his partner, you were:

THE MOST UNCOUTH LOOKING YOUNG MAN I EVER SAW. [HE] SEEMED TO HAVE BUT LITTLE TO SAY; SEEMED TO FEEL TIMID, WITH A TINGE OF SADNESS VISIBLE IN THE COUNTENANCE, BUT WHEN HE DID TALK ALL OF THIS DISAPPEARED FOR THE TIME AND HE DEMONSTRATED THAT HE WAS BOTH STRONG AND ACUTE. . . . HE SURPRISED US MORE AND MORE AT EVERY VISIT.

In 1836, you not only won a second term but also got named floor leader for the assembly's Whigs, quite a vote of confidence for a twenty-seven-year-old. Still, an even younger man attracted more attention: Stephen A. Douglas, Democrat, age twenty-three. He was about a foot shorter than you, but his keen intelligence, deep voice, and imposing mane soon earned him the nickname the Little Giant. Get used to it: you'll be seeing a lot more of him.

Abe's best frenemy.

STEPHEN DOUGLAS

From your leadership position, you pushed for "internal improvements," major infrastructure projects such as railroads, bridges, and canals. Given your faith in human and social progress, such public works will always be a top priority for you. You also convinced the assembly to select Springfield as the new state capital, effective 1839; little Vandalia just could not grow fast enough to accommodate the ballooning state government. In April 1837, you moved to Springfield yourself; not only would the assembly be meeting there soon, but you also had your law license and an offer to join Stuart's firm as a junior partner.

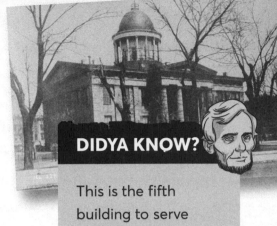

SPRINGING AHEAD IN SPRINGFIELD

SPRINGFIELD WAS large for Illinois, but it was no metropolis. The streets were dirt, which made the many hogs that roamed them very happy when it rained.

When you became one of the 1,500 or so inhabitants, you were so poor you couldn't even pay up front for bed linens. You walked into Joshua Speed's general store and promised to pay him in eight months if your law practice succeeded, adding with customary honesty, "If I fail in that I will probably never be able to pay you at all."

Speed had never seen "so gloomy and melancholy a face" in his life, but felt he could trust you. He offered to save you the expense altogether by letting you take half of his own big bed upstairs; although he was five years younger, he came from a wealthy Kentucky family and could afford to be generous. You immediately accepted and have shared lodgings with him to this day (1840), forming a deep and lifelong friendship.

Most evenings, people came to Speed's store to sit around the fire and swap stories, especially if they knew you were going to be there. Several young lawyers were among the regulars, including Douglas, with whom you often had spirited discussions on policy. As it happens, you faced off against Douglas in your first criminal court case, in which he was prosecuting an accused murderer whom you succeeded in getting acquitted. Chalk one up for you!

Most of your practice was commercial, though: disputes over land purchases, lawsuits over a hog or a batch of flour, and the like.

You quickly established a reputation as a careful researcher and writer, though your senior partner, Stuart, usually argued the cases. When he won election to Congress in 1838 (barely beating Douglas), he was happy to have you carry on without him, though he still collected his share of the fees. This year (1840) Stuart was reelected, so you and he agreed to part ways, leaving you free to join Stephen Logan's practice, still as a junior partner (though you'd previously won all three of the cases in which you'd faced off against Logan).

No Short Circuits Here!

SINCE **STUART LEFT IN 1838**, you've been spending part of each year traveling the state judicial system's Eighth Circuit for your practice. The circuit covers Springfield's own Sangamon County, which is huge (about half the size of Rhode Island), plus fourteen other counties in central Illinois. The population is too sparse to support full-time courts in each county, so twice each year a motley band of lawyers and a judge travel around the circuit. They gather in each county seat for a few days or a week, until the local cases have been decided, and then pack up their briefs (their legal papers), heading on to the next county.

You enjoy the companionship of life on the road, and you've made many friends around the fires of small inns and farmhouses along the way.

Your circuit jaunts have let many people

Who brought s'mores?

enjoy your "inexhaustible fund" of funny stories and, more important, have greatly widened your political connections.

The speeches you've been giving wherever you can have expanded your reputation further. An important one was to the Young Men's Lyceum (a kind of discussion club) in Springfield. It was published in the county paper and will one day be praised for its foresight. You cautioned that America, while protected by oceans from any foreign invaders, was still vulnerable to strife from within: "If destruction be our lot, we must ourselves be its author and finisher. As a nation of freemen, we must live through all time, or die by suicide."

That speech, in January 1838, helped you win a third assembly term, and you've just been elected to a fourth. Congrats!

You're now one of the leading Whigs in Illinois and still only thirty-one. That's an impressive age for a four-term legislator, but you're actually behind most politicians in another important milestone: finding a wife. In a time when family men are seen by most voters as steadier and more reliable, your single status could put your career at risk.

BORN TO COMMAND.

OF VETO MEMORY.

KING ANDREW THE FIRST.

FUN FACT

The Whig Party was not a fake-hair festival! It formed mostly out of loathing for President Andrew Jackson, whom the Whigs mockingly called King Andrew.

(NOT SO) LUCKY IN LOVE

IT'S NOT THAT YOU HAVEN'T *tried* to get married. A year after your heartbreak over Ann Rutledge, you had a brief engagement to Mary Owens, but it seems you were never really that into each other. One fateful day, you and she went riding with some other couples, and you came to a stream. The other men each waited for their dates to cross safely before riding on, but you dashed ahead without checking that Mary was okay. Later you tried to excuse your thoughtlessness, saying, "You're plenty smart to take care of yourself." Smooth move, Romeo.

In Mary Owens's judgment, "Mr. Lincoln was deficient in those little links which make up the great chain of a woman's happiness."

For your part, you were having second thoughts about her "want of teeth, weatherbeaten appearance ... and present bulk" (not that *you're* such a looker). So neither of

I am not impressed.

MARY OWENS

you was too upset when the relationship ended. You weren't really much of a catch anyway, you wrote to a friend: "I have now come to the conclusion never again to think of marrying, and for this reason: I can never be satisfied with anyone who would be blockhead enough to have me."

Your outlook changed last year, though, when you

met a pretty Kentuckian named Mary Todd. She's staying with her sister Elizabeth Edwards, who lives in one of Springfield's finest houses, having married the son of a former Illinois governor. Mary's the center of a fashionable Springfield clique, and she's already caught the eye of several eligible bachelors (including Stephen Douglas, whose proposal she'll someday tell a friend she turned down).

Mary Todd's family home—nothing like the log cabins where Abe was raised.

You first spotted Mary at a dance party at the Edwards mansion, where you wore typical Lincoln duds—patched trousers and mismatched socks.

You saw her delicate features, petite five-foot-two

figure, blue eyes, and soft brown hair, and told her, "Miss Todd, I want to dance with you in the worst way."

"And he certainly did," she later joked to a cousin. But since that evening, the two of you have been spending a *lot* of time together.

WHAT DOES SHE SEE IN YOU?

KIND OF SURPRISING, WHEN YOU think about it. Springfield is about two-thirds male, a typical frontier town, so Mary's got many other options. Coming from a wealthy family, she has plenty of suitors better educated and handsomer than you. You're older than Mary by nine years yet still haven't managed to refine your manners much: at another party where the ladies are wearing silk gowns, you stomp in (boots muddy, pants too short) and exclaim, "Oh boys, how clean these girls look!" Somehow, though, Mary can see the strong character behind your unsightly exterior (her sister calls you "the plainest man" in Springfield), and she likes what she sees.

Despite your differences, you and Mary have much in common. You both value learning: Mary's dad believed in education for his daughters, if only to make them better wives and mothers.

Sent away to fancy schools, Mary out-shone the other stu-dents and now knows French, Latin, liter-ature, history—more than most women she'll ever meet. More than many men, too, which did not please the Southern gents with whom she often argued

Mary had a taste for the fancy.

MARY TODD LINCOLN

politics at home. She would end up winning the argu-ments but losing chances for dates, one reason she's not in Kentucky anymore.

Like you, Mary lost her mom at a young age (Mary was only six). Unfortunately, Mary's stepmother was a witch who preferred her own kids and habitually called the girl a limb of Satan. It took seven generations to make a lady, the snooty woman announced soon after meeting Mary, and Mary was six generations short. Her stepmother is clearly another reason Mary left home.

Like you, Mary disapproves of slavery; you've been on the record as being against it for years. Although her family had plenty of slaves, she hates the system. She grew up seeing black people marched by cruel slavers past the Todds' front door, dragged in chains to the auction block downtown. She often heard her Whig father say slavery shouldn't spread to any additional states. (The Democratic Party, by contrast, generally favors slavery's expansion into newly created states and ultimately into free states such as Indiana and Illinois.)

When Mary was only twelve, her treasured Mammy Sally (a slave and by then her only source of motherly love) confided that runaway slaves were

> **FUN FACT**
>
> In Abe's day, Republicans were liberal and Democrats were conservative. Today, not so much!

sometimes fed in the family's kitchen on their way north.

Also like you, Mary has big dreams. She grew up near Henry Clay, the great statesman who founded the Whig Party. When she heard as a girl that he was running for president, she told him she wished *she* could go to Washington and live in the White House. Clay didn't win, but Mary has since expressed hopes of one day being married to a president—and, with your intelligence and integrity, she believes it might be you.

You think she's quite terrific herself. Her sister Elizabeth's husband says Mary is pretty and spirited enough to "make a bishop forget his prayers." Elizabeth will recall that when you visited, "Mary led the conversation—Lincoln would listen and gaze on her as if drawn by some superior power."

HENRY CLAY

THE CHOICE

YOU AND MARY HAVE BEEN together more than a year now and are informally engaged, but are you ready for marriage? You're not sure. Your prospects are still cloudy, as Mary's family likes to remind her, and you haven't finished paying off the debts left over from your failed store. If you aren't 100 percent positive, should you be continuing this relationship? Where can you turn for advice?

WHAT DO YOU DO, ABRAHAM? SELECT ONE:

A. Break up with Mary.

Mary is a catch, but are you ready to get married? You don't know how your career will progress, and you're not yet financially stable because you still have debt to pay off. Having a wife might limit your ability to travel on business, your freedom to stay up late reading, and your flexibility to follow your career wherever it may lead. Beyond that, you're still not positive Mary is the one for you. If you aren't certain, should you stay in the relationship? On the other hand, you do love her. Given more time, you could see yourself growing to love her more. Should you act on your doubts when you could be giving up something valuable?

B. Date other women.

If you're really not sure Mary is your one and only, maybe you should play the field and see if meeting other women will bring you clarity. However, honor is everything to you, and dating others might disrespect Mary. "I want in all cases to do right," you've written, "and most particularly so, in all cases with women." Also, there's no one else you're interested in (and probably vice versa) right now. Still, could it hurt to look around a little?

C. Marry fast, before your feet get even colder.

If you were to get married, would you really want to do it this way? A rushed wedding might not look good. On the other hand, you *think* you love Mary. Do you want to take the chance that your doubts will drive her away forever?

D. Consult a pastor.

As it happens, you're not big on religion. You have never formally joined a church, and you never will. You haven't even attended many services since childhood, when your Baptist parents dragged you along. (Afterward, you would amuse your friends with pitch-perfect parodies of the sermons, delivered from a tree stump.) You also don't believe in an afterlife, which robs you of some comfort when you think about the loved ones you've lost.

Nevertheless, you do try to live a spiritual life:

★ You know much of the Bible by heart, and not just as literature. For instance, you take seriously its lesson about the Good Samaritan, who helped an injured stranger by the road. When you and a friend were coming home late one frigid night in Indiana, you found a man lying drunk in a half-frozen mudhole. You knew he would die if he stayed there much longer, but you couldn't wake him up. Your friend watched you lift the drunkard up and carry him home, tending him by the fire all night until you were sure he'd be okay.

★ You do not drink alcohol; your favorite beverage is water, which you sometimes call Adam's ale. Nor do you gamble, smoke, or curse.

★ You believe firmly in a superior being, whom you often call God or the Almighty. You want to do

God's will, even if you don't feel certainty about any one religious denomination's views. Your doctrine is more basic: "When I do good I feel good, when I do bad I feel bad, and that's my religion."

★ Your speeches and writing will often show a sense of destiny, of a plan beyond the understanding of human beings. It may be this sense of a higher power that helps you to withstand some of the tragedies in your life, to feel real human fellowship even with those who disagree with you, and to keep your sense of mission despite the many obstacles placed in your path.

For a spiritual man like you, marriage is an especially important and difficult decision. An outside perspective, especially from someone who has conducted many weddings and observed the results, could be extremely useful. Many people use pastors as trusted advisors; they could certainly hold some form of "holy" insight that you don't have. Is it finally time to turn toward religion for answers?

THE REVEAL

YOU CHOSE . . . **A. Break up with Mary.** It seems the only right thing to do. You can't marry without being (in Joshua Speed's words) "entirely satisfied that his *heart* was going with his hand." You consult Speed, not a pastor, showing him a "Dear Mary" letter you've written. Speed wisely advises that such news is best delivered in person.

The conversation does not go according to plan. When you say that maybe the two of you shouldn't marry after all, Mary starts crying. "To tell you the truth, Speed," you report later, "it was too much for me. I felt the tears trickling down my own cheeks. I caught her in my arms and kissed her." But the damage is done; on January 1, 1841 (the Fatal First, you'll call it), she sends *you* a letter giving you the freedom you wanted. No doubt her family is influencing her to back away from you.

THE AFTERMATH

THE BREAKUP SENDS YOU TUMBLING into depression—"crazy as a loon," one friend will say.

You're absent from the assembly for six consecutive days, a first for you, then show up "reduced and emaciated," writes one colleague, "and [he] seems scarcely to possess strength enough to speak above a whisper." Speed is so worried about your state of mind that he hides your razors so you won't harm yourself. You write to Stuart in Washington:

> *I am now the most miserable man living. If what I feel were equally distributed to the whole human family, there would not be one cheerful face on the earth. . . . Whether I shall ever be better I cannot tell; I awfully forebode I shall not. To remain as I am is impossible; I must die or be better, it appears to me.*

Of course, Stuart happens to be another of Mary's cousins (his middle name is Todd). Could you perhaps be hoping he'll pass on to her how awful you feel?

You don't date others even after the breakup. Mary, for her part, considers seeing other men, including a lawyer and friend of yours named Lyman Trumbull (more on him later). But (lucky for you) she can't bring herself to think seriously of anyone else while you're still a possibility.

In 1842, a female friend invites you and Mary to her parlor, not telling either the other is coming. Your hostess says you and Mary should at least be friends, so you start conversing (naturally) about politics. From there you move on to poetry, from which it's a short step to deciding that it might be a good idea to start seeing each other again. Her family looks down on you, so you keep the meetings a secret.

Next you get to show your love for Mary with a romantic gesture. She and her dear friend Julia Jayne (who will end up marrying Lyman Trumbull) write an anonymous satire in the town paper against a Democratic politician named James Shields. Judging by the piece's sly humor, he assumes *you* wrote it. You don't betray Mary's secret—not even when Shields challenges you to a duel!

Luckily, no one gets hurt. As the challenged party, you get to pick weapons, so you go for cavalry swords, which favor your greater height. After a few harmless swipes, both sides declare honor satisfied and retire from the field. No doubt Mary is grateful for your chivalry, because your relationship continues to deepen until, one morning in November 1842, you each announce that you are marrying that very day.

Mary's family is furious, doing their best to change her mind. (They throw around terms like "white trash," but let's not dwell on that.) When they realize Mary is determined, Elizabeth decides she can't let her sister marry in someone else's house, so the private ceremony takes place in her living room.

The ring you give Mary is inscribed LOVE IS ETERNAL—which in your case turns out to be true. Your marriage, in its own way, is going to work. Each of you is unconventional, each allows the other to break a few of society's rules, and each fits almost uncannily with the other's emotional needs—as the twenty-three years to come will show.

SOUTH OF
WHICH
BORDER?

THE CHALLENGE

YOU'RE MARRIED NOW, WITH CHILDREN, and you've made it into Congress. The president has launched a war against Mexico, which the United States is about to win. Most voters approve, but you think this war is wrong. What do you do?

THE BACKSTORY

PERSONAL STUFF FIRST. **MARY MARRIED** you knowing she was taking a huge social step down. Her family (even her sister Elizabeth) had little to do with her for years afterward, their anger at her mixing with their disdain for you. When you began your married life in a room above a tavern because it was cheap, Mary did not complain about the change to her lifestyle. It was only after the birth in 1843 of Robert, your first child, that you rented a cottage. The next year, having finally paid off your debts, you managed to buy a small house (the only home you'll ever own).

LIFE WITH (AND WITHOUT) ABE

BEING MRS. LINCOLN HAS NOT been easy, especially for a woman raised in Southern luxury. You can't afford more than a servant or two, so she has tons of housework to do, especially after the arrival in 1846 of your second son, Edward. With you still traveling the court circuit six months a year, she has to do most chores herself. (A neighbor will recall her often saying that "if her husband had stayed at home as he ought to, she could love him better.") Her tasks are endless: caring for the boys, cleaning the house, keeping the fire going, pumping water, preserving fruit, baking twice a week, milking the cow (once you can afford one), making butter and cheese, sewing and washing clothes for the whole family, and on and on.

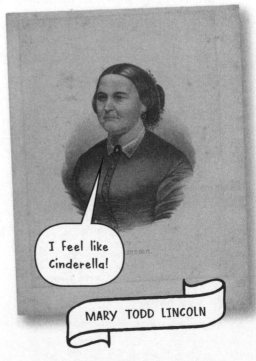

I feel like Cinderella!

MARY TODD LINCOLN

Here's one way women handle the ever-present cockroach problem, for instance: boil up some pokeberry roots, put them with molasses into dishes, leave them out overnight, then scrape the sticky mixture (now covered with roaches) into the garbage each morning. Good times.

Mary has to kill the chickens for family dinners herself. Actually, chicken is an improvement over the meats you two started out eating, such as game birds and woodchuck. You yourself don't have much taste for food, often barely remembering what you just ate, so she doesn't get the appreciation for her cooking that many wives do. Then again, no one ever taught her to cook (or thought she'd ever *need* to cook), so your indifference to food may be just as well.

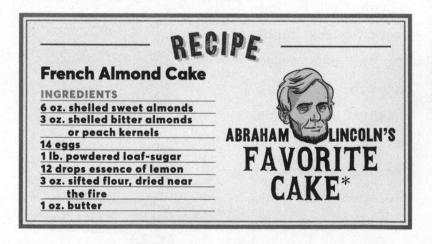

RECIPE

French Almond Cake

INGREDIENTS

6 oz. shelled sweet almonds
3 oz. shelled bitter almonds
    or peach kernels
14 eggs
1 lb. powdered loaf-sugar
12 drops essence of lemon
3 oz. sifted flour, dried near
    the fire
1 oz. butter

ABRAHAM LINCOLN'S
FAVORITE CAKE*

Mrs. Lincoln's Famous French Almond Cake*

While not particularly talented in the kitchen, Mary Todd did have one culinary creation that delighted the future president's taste buds. Her French almond cake was a hit, **AND ABE ONCE SAID IT WAS THE BEST CAKE HE EVER ATE.**

DIRECTIONS

Blanch the almonds by scalding them in hot water. Put them in a bowl of cold water, and wipe them dry when you take them out. Pound them, one at a time, in a mortar, until they are perfectly smooth. Mix the sweet and bitter almonds together. Prepare them, if possible, the day before the cake is made. (While pounding the almonds, pour in occasionally a little rosewater. It makes them much lighter.)

Put the whites and yolks of the eggs into separate pans. Beat the whites until they stand alone, and then the yolks until they are very thick.

Add the sugar gradually to the yolks, beating it in very hard. Add, by degrees, the almonds, still beating very hard. Then put in the essence of lemon. Next, beat in gradually the whites of the eggs, continuing to beat for some time after they are all in. Lastly, stir in the flour, as slowly and lightly as possible.

Butter a large tin mold or pan. Put the cake in and bake it in a very quick oven, an hour or more according to its thickness. The oven must on no account be hotter at the top than at the bottom.

When done, set it on a sieve to cool. Ice it, and ornament it with nonpareils. These almond cakes are generally baked in a bundt tin, and the nonpareils put on in spots or sprigs.

A pound of almonds in the shells (if the shells are soft and thin) will generally yield half a pound when shelled. Hard, thick-shelled almonds seldom yield much more than a quarter of a pound, and should therefore never be bought for cakes or puddings.

Bitter almonds and peach kernels can always be purchased with the shells off. Families should always save their peach kernels, as they can be used in cakes, puddings, and custards.

*Okay, this isn't *exactly* Mary Todd's French almond cake recipe, but it was adapted from *Seventy-Five Receipts for Pastry, Cakes, and Sweetmeats* by Miss Leslie, of Philadelphia, in 1832, and would have been similar to recipes found in cookbooks Mary Todd would have used.

You've never paid much attention to your clothes, but now you've got Mary to do it for you. Though you've gradually improved, she's often scandalized by your inability to put an outfit together or keep it clean. "Why don't you dress up and try to look like somebody?" she often pleads.

You two still have your books in common, at least: you spend quiet evenings reading together—sometimes to each other—and she loves reading to the kids, now that they're old enough. Nor is Mary too busy to encourage your political career, still predicting a brilliant future for you. "But nobody knows me," you sometimes tell her. "They soon will," she assures you. You call her "my dearest partner of greatness."

COMPETE FOR THE SEAT

GREATNESS ELUDED YOU IN 1842, when your former partner John Stuart announced he would not be running for a third term in Congress. You began competing for his seat, along with two other Whigs, John Hardin (yet another cousin of Mary's) and Edward Baker. They were both lawyers and state legislators, both Black Hawk War veterans, and both friends of yours. Whoever got the Whig nomination would most likely go to Washington, because yours is the one Illinois congressional district in which Whigs outnumber Democrats.

You campaigned hard but had two major disadvantages. First, some people thought you were godless because you belonged to no congregation; it didn't help that Mary went to the Episcopalian church, seen as a bit hoity-toity. Second, Mary's family was so rich that voters suspected you would represent the moneyed classes, a mistake you found highly ironic as a recent "friendless, uneducated, penniless boy."

Once you realized you couldn't win, you not only withdrew but also agreed to become chairman of Baker's delegation at the nominating convention. You wrote to Speed that "in getting Baker the nomination, I shall be 'fixed' a good deal like a fellow who is made groomsman to the man what has cut him out, and is marrying his own dear 'gal.'" In the end Hardin

FUN FACT

Abe and Mary named their second son Edward Baker Lincoln, after Abe's opponent and friend.

won, but you persuaded the delegates that Baker should be nominated the next time around. This rotation idea helped Baker in 1844, but it wasn't completely selfless: you clearly had 1846 in mind for yourself.

MR. SENIOR PARTNER

IN THE MEANTIME, YOU FOCUSED on expanding your network (and net worth) through the practice of law. Your senior partner, Logan, brought his son on in 1844, so you decided it was time to start your own firm. Now *you* needed a junior partner, and you chose William Herndon, whose father owns a Springfield hotel.

Herndon is nine years younger than you and once worked at Speed's store, where he shared the upstairs room with you and Speed. Now he's got a college degree and a law license, for which he prepared by working for you and Logan. "Billy, do you want to enter into a partnership with me?" you asked him out of the blue. "I can trust you, if you can trust me."

He does trust you—and respects you, calling you Mr. Lincoln. As senior partner, you argue most of the cases, but you give Herndon half the firm's profits, even though as a junior partner *you* got only a third. Neither of you is very well organized: your shared office is a mess, with dust covering everything. How much dust? So much that grass seeds actually take root once between the floorboards.

Stacks of paper cover the floor as well, including one in the corner, labeled in your handwriting, "If you can't find it anywhere else, look in here."

ORGANIZATION TIPS FROM ABE

1. Store your planner in your hat—that way you'll never leave home without it!
2. Don't worry about soil on the floor; you'll have a wonderful garden there come spring.
3. Forget dirty dishes; used mugs make excellent pencil holders.
4. It's perfectly acceptable to consider the floor one giant shelf.

You often keep notes in the lining of your stovepipe hat, a tall black cylinder (in beaver fur) that accentuates your height. Herndon will recall that your hat often looked as if "a calf had just licked it," but it was "an extraordinary receptacle. It was his desk and his memorandum book."

Although Herndon will call you "a riddle and a puzzle to his neighbors," he will come to understand and describe you better than most: "His structure was loose and leathery. . . . The whole man, body and mind, worked slowly, as if it needed oiling."

He will also recall about you that "his melancholy dripped from him as he walked."

You do admit to "a tendency to melancholy," which you call "a misfortune not a fault." You look even gloomier in photos, though. In these early days of photography, portraits require subjects to sit still for long exposures.

Don't tell me to say "cheese."

Expressions come out so stiff and unnatural that Mary can tease you out of bad moods by laughing that you look as if you're having your picture taken.

Your many photos (the first one taken in 1846) cannot show how lively your face becomes once you're in conversation. In the words of one reporter, "The dull, listless features dropped like a mask. The eyes began to sparkle, the mouth to smile, the whole countenance was wreathed in animation, so that a stranger would have said, 'Why, this man, so angular and solemn a moment ago, is really handsome!'"

A Congressional Comedian

YOU'RE GETTING A LOT MORE press these days, now that you're in Washington. (Herndon: "His ambition was a little engine that knew no rest.")

Yes, you got the Whig nomination in 1846, as you'd hoped, then faced a fiery preacher named Peter Cartwright in the general election. You knew the Democrats would try to use his religious credentials

I think I can.
I think I can.

THE EXPRESS TRAIN.

against you, so you preempted them with a handbill explaining:

> THAT I AM NOT A MEMBER OF ANY CHRISTIAN CHURCH, IS TRUE; BUT I HAVE NEVER DENIED THE TRUTH OF THE SCRIPTURES; AND I HAVE NEVER SPOKEN WITH INTENTIONAL DISRESPECT OF RELIGION IN GENERAL, OR OF ANY DENOMINATION OF CHRISTIANS IN PARTICULAR. . . . I DO NOT THINK I COULD MYSELF BE BROUGHT TO SUPPORT A MAN FOR OFFICE, WHOM I KNEW TO BE AN OPEN ENEMY OF, AND SCOFFER AT, RELIGION.

You even attended one of Cartwright's sermons, during which he suddenly demanded that everyone who wished to go to Heaven should stand up. Most of the audience rose to their feet. When he told all those who didn't want to go to Hell that they should also stand, you were the only one left sitting. Cartwright glared at you. "May I inquire of you, Mr. Lincoln, where are you going?" Your response, an instant classic, helped you win the election by a broader margin than either Hardin's or Baker's: "If it's all the same to you, I am going to Congress."

And go you did. Of the $200 you raised for your campaign, you returned $199.25, explaining that you rode your own horse, stayed with friends, and spent only "75 cents for a barrel of cider, which some farmhands insisted I should treat to."

The town paper sent you off in style: "Success to our talented member of Congress! He will find many men in Congress who possess twice the good looks, and not half the good sense, of our own representative."

Now you, Mary, and the boys are installed at a boardinghouse in which eight other Whig congressmen are also living. Shared meals are boisterous events (partly thanks to you) that Mary usually skips, preferring to stay in your room. Most of the other lodgers are there without families, and Mary will soon decide to head home with the boys. In the meantime, she does enjoy DC's many opportunities for shopping, a pastime she will relish more and more over the years. Washington, with more than 35,000 people (including 8,000 slaves), is much larger than Springfield, but it shares some of the same problems: unpaved streets, roaming pigs, and pitiful sanitation. There are cowsheds by the Capitol.

THE CHOICE

THE MAJOR POLITICAL ISSUE OF the session is the Mexican War. President James Polk declared it over a land dispute in 1846, just a year after the United

States annexed the formerly Mexican territory of Texas. The war's battles are now finished (the United States has pretty much won), but the treaty is still being negotiated. Many Whigs (including your political hero Henry Clay) opposed the war, partly because they feared slavery could spread westward into any territories won from Mexico. Now, even though the fighting's over, the war and its possible peace terms continue to ignite shouting matches in Congress.

You could adopt your party's position, insisting that the war is a dangerous land grab. On the other hand, most of Illinois votes Democratic, and even some Whigs in your district like the idea of using this treaty to continue western expansion. If you take a strong stand against the war or attack the president's policy, it could hurt you in Illinois. A no-win situation?

WHAT DO YOU DO, ABRAHAM? SELECT ONE:

A. Keep quiet.
You know a trap when you see one. The Democrats have introduced resolutions blessing Polk's war, calling

it justified by Mexican aggression. Why the backward-looking move? Because they *want* to provoke you Whigs into taking an unpopular political stand.

You don't have to fall for their trick. You're quite capable of measured tones; in one congressional speech, you say, "The true rule, in determining to embrace or reject any thing, is not whether it have *any* evil in it; but whether it have more of evil, than of good." Your legal training has taught you to be careful, sometimes even saying things like "I am almost ready to say this is probably true."

B. Support the war and the president.

You disagree with both. Polk claims that Mexico started the war by attacking an American patrol on US territory, but in fact the incident happened on a disputed strip of land between the Nueces River and the (farther south) Rio Grande. America had been making aggressive moves for years before, such as annexing Texas (which had declared its independence from Mexico), sending an armed force under John C. Frémont into Mexico's California territory, and ordering troops into that disputed "Nueces Strip." So who *really* started this war? Still, it would be more politic for you and your party not to challenge Polk on this sensitive topic.

C. Support the war, attack the president.

Most voters love the war, because America is gaining victory and land. Perhaps you could criticize the president for how he fought the war, or for how he justified it, without denouncing the war itself. That way you might make your mark in Congress and give the Democrats a black eye, while not making yourself unpopular with your political base.

D. Attack the war and the president.

This is what you'd really like to do, but is it wise? Even some Whigs are applauding Polk for beating the Mexicans and expanding the United States. The train has left the station, Abraham. You may not have the heart to jump on board, but do you really want to throw yourself in front of it?

THE REVEAL

YOU CHOSE . . . **D. Attack the war and the president.** You don't care if the Democrats' justification of an almost-over conflict is a trap. You despise the president's war so heartily that you don't feel you can remain quiet.

Also, you didn't get elected just to play it safe. So you decide it's time to make your mark in this Congress. You write home to your law partner, Herndon: "As you are all so anxious for me to distinguish myself, I have concluded to do so, before long."

You think President Polk started this war, not the Mexicans. You're also against war in general: you call military glory "that attractive rainbow that rises in showers of blood." This particular war you consider "immoral and unnecessary." Most Americans are pleased to be winning so much territory; the final treaty will grant the United States the whole swath from Texas to California, a region nearly the size of Western Europe. But you and other Whigs worry that the new land will suffer the same taint of slavery that stains the existing Southern states.

You *claim* you're supporting the army, because you do vote to send the supplies it needs. But no one is fooled: you consider this a war of US aggression. You introduce a series of resolutions demanding facts from Polk, in particular whether "the spot" where the first battle occurred was really US territory then. You use the word "spot" so often, these become known as the Spot Resolutions. Newspapers begin calling you "spotty Lincoln."

To you, this is "Mr. Polk's war," and you heap on the scorn. You call him a "bewildered, confounded, and miserably perplexed man" and describe his war message as "the half insane mumbling of a fever-dream," which shows his mind "running hither and thither, like some tortured creature, on a burning surface, finding no position, on which it can settle down, and be at ease." Harsh!

THE AFTERMATH

EVEN MANY **WHIGS** FIND YOUR disrespect to a sitting president shocking, and Illinois Democrats go ballistic. "Out, damned Spot!" shrieks one newspaper there, while another calls you a traitor, "a second Benedict Arnold."

You defend yourself: accepting Polk's excuses would "allow the President to invade a nation

Welcome to the club, Abe.

BENEDICT ARNOLD

whenever . . . he says it is necessary." Still, your choice to attack Polk pretty much stops your political career in its tracks. Not only will you never again be elected to the House of Representatives, but many also blame you when the next Whig candidate for your seat (your old partner Stephen Logan) loses to a Democrat.

You should have known better, Abraham. You're perfectly aware that respect and dignity win more arguments than insults do. Nowhere have you made that clearer than in an 1842 speech you gave to an Illinois temperance (anti-liquor) society. One can't hope to reform drunkards by insulting and criticizing them, you said: "If you would win a man to your cause, *first* convince him that you are his sincere friend." As you mature politically, you will remember this important lesson more often.

DEADLOCK!

THE CHALLENGE

STANDING ON PRINCIPLE AGAINST THE Mexican War has already damaged you politically. Now, just as your hopes for office are reviving, you face another tough choice. Which do you put first: your recovering political career or the fight against slavery?

THE BACKSTORY

YOU SPENT THE FALL OF 1848 campaigning in Massachusetts for Zachary Taylor, the Whig candidate for president. In New England, at least, you were not damaged political goods.

Taylor's politics were unclear, and he was a Southern slaveholder. On the plus side, he was a war hero and thus electable. In the end, Taylor won but died after a year and four months in the White House, to be succeeded by the moderate Whig Millard Fillmore.

Your campaigning achieved a couple of other things. First, it threw you together with William H. Seward, a former New York governor—also stumping for Taylor—who will play a major role in your life. Second, it earned you Taylor's gratitude and the offer to appoint you governor of the Oregon Territory. You turned him down, though, because

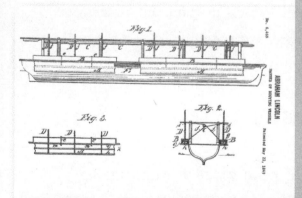

DIDYA KNOW?

Abe is the only president to own a patent. Inspired by his time on the river as a young man, Abe developed a buoy system to help boats navigate over sandbars. Ahoy, Cap'n Abe!

Mary had no interest in moving farther west. You also expected Oregon to lean Democratic once it became a state—not very promising for you politically.

As if *Illinois* were promising! Given the widespread anger at your performance in Congress, you decided to practice law full-time. Your partner, William Herndon, offered you half the fees he'd earned while you were in Washington, but you refused to take money for work in which you'd played no part (unlike John Stuart, who'd been happy to keep profiting off you while *he* served in Congress). You were wistful about leaving politics behind, telling Herndon, "How hard, oh how hard it is to die and leave one's country no better than if one had never lived."

You may have been out of politics, but politics wasn't out of *you*. You followed it incredibly closely. You would come into the office early most mornings, spread your lanky frame across an old leather couch, and read newspapers from all over the country—not only the Whig papers but also Southern dailies. To Herndon you explained, "Let us have both sides at the table. Each is entitled to its day in court."

You tracked the negotiations (led by your idol Henry Clay) that produced the famous Compromise of 1850, which resolved the ongoing dispute about slavery in the new southwestern territories.

California was established as a free state, while the rest could decide their own status by popular vote. Also, the slave trade was outlawed in DC, in return for which the newly passed Fugitive Slave Act made it much easier for slaveholders to reclaim runaways who'd reached the North.

Stephen Douglas, now a Democratic senator, helped the bills get passed. His career has left yours in the dust: appointed to the Illinois Supreme Court in 1841 (age twenty-seven!), elected to the House of Representatives in 1843 and the Senate in 1847, and now a leader of the Democratic Party.

Meanwhile, you've mostly focused on law, arguing more than a hundred cases in Springfield and on the court circuit over the five years since you left Congress. These represented a lot of effort, given how slowly and thoroughly you work: "I am never easy, when I am handling a thought, till I have bounded it North, and bounded it South, and bounded it East, and bounded it West." In Herndon's words, you "not only went to the root of the question, but dug up the root, and separated and analyzed every fiber of it." As a result, opponents judging you by your laid-back manner were often surprised. Leonard Swett, a close colleague from the circuit, will remember that "any man who took Lincoln for a simple-minded man would very soon wake up with his back in a ditch."

Your intellectual curiosity doesn't end with the law: lately you've also been perusing Euclid (the ancient mathematician) and rereading the Bible.

According to Swett, "Life to [Lincoln] was a school, and he was always studying and mastering every subject which came before him." There's no question that your thirst for knowledge makes you a better attorney.

In 1850, you drafted a guide for young lawyers. Although you never published it, it reveals much about you as a person. Along with standard advice—work hard and practice speechmaking—you recommended never bringing suit unless absolutely necessary.

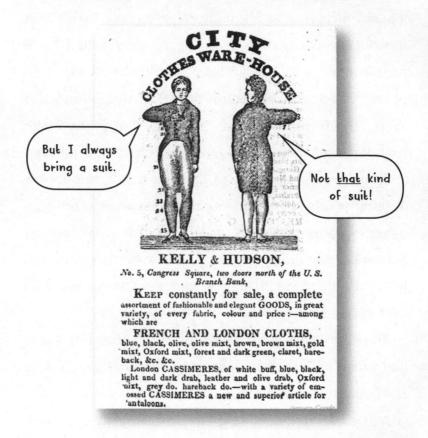

Make sure your clients understand, you said, that peace through bargaining may be cheaper than pursuing cases to the end, even if they should win. (You walk your talk here, once even writing to a client that if he chose to settle, "I will charge nothing for what I have done, and thank you to boot.") Most important, you say, young lawyers must disprove the popular belief that lawyers are crooked: "Resolve to be honest at all events; and if, in your own judgment, you cannot be an honest lawyer, resolve to be honest without being a lawyer."

CIRCUIT BREAKS

YOUR WORK ON THE CIRCUIT takes you through an area of about 15,000 square miles, larger than all of Connecticut. You're no longer riding your five hundred or so miles (twice a year!) on horseback, instead hitching "Old Buck" to a buggy, rain or shine.

Your friend Judge David Davis, at three hundred pounds, needs *two* horses for his wagon.

You, Davis, and Swett make a steady trio along the circuit, and they (with Herndon) will also form the core of your political support team when that time comes. Every successful candidate needs good friends, and yours (let's call them FOAs, for Friends of Abraham) will prove themselves more steadfast than any other politician's.

Unlike most circuit lawyers, you visit every county every time, not even heading home for weekends. Your devotion to the circuit causes some tension with Mary—or is it the other way around? According

Friends of Abe, unite!

JUDGE DAVID DAVIS

to Herndon, "his home was *Hell.* . . . Absence from home was his *Heaven.*" Then again, Herndon never did like Mary, and few people understand the bond that exists between you and her.

Hijinks at Home

MARY IS, TO PUT IT mildly, high-strung. She is now the stressed-out mother of three boys: Bobbie, Willie, and Tad. (Poor Eddie did not live to see his fourth birthday.) She often takes her frustrations out on you, hurling potatoes or even chasing you with a kitchen knife. You generally just laugh and walk away. Once, when you ignore her repeated requests to put another log in the hearth, she bops you on the nose with a piece of firewood. When people ask why you tolerate such treatment, you say, "It does her lots of good, and it doesn't hurt me a bit." Your philosophy seems to work: no matter how upset she gets, the two of you always make up.

Motherhood comes hard to Mary: she sometimes alarms the neighbors by screaming that one kid or another is missing, or dying, or murdered, when the situation is not nearly so serious. She hates to discipline the boys, no matter how much the neighbors complain about their mischief; she insists they're "the noblest, purest, most talented ever given to parents."

You refuse to beat the boys yourself, unusual for this era; perhaps you're determined not to be the kind of dad you had. "We never controlled our children much," you'll admit, and so they're growing up out of control. When Willie was four, he once jumped out of the bathtub and ran naked into the street. Luckily, you were sitting on the front porch, so you chased him down with your long stride, plopped him on your shoulders, and carried him home. Not even a swat to punish him— you were laughing too hard.

You're a doting father, sometimes pulling your sons around the block in a toy wagon. You often perform this task, like your plowing in the old days, with your nose in a book. You trudge along, reading while you tow the cart behind you, barely noticing your surroundings—even when Tad falls out one time and you don't notice until Mary hears him bawling and calls you back.

Like Father, *Not* Like Son

YOU NEVER LET YOUR OWN dad, who died in 1851, meet Mary or the boys, though he sent letters saying he "craved" to see his "only child." You loved your stepmom, but whatever wounds you felt from him could not heal. When he got sick in 1850, you offered help with money or doctors but refused to visit, because "if we could meet now, it is doubtful whether it would not be more painful than pleasant." You didn't even attend his funeral the next year. He left you his eighty-acre farm, but you had no interest in anything from him, selling it to your stepbrother for a dollar. It's a shame things had to end that way.

Busy as you've been, you will look back on these years outside politics as a relatively quiet time in your life. Now, though, politics is reclaiming you. Guess who's to thank? Your old rival Stephen Douglas.

So, Douglas. We meet again.

ABRAHAM LINCOLN

STEPHEN DOUGLAS

The Douglas Debacle

REELECTED EASILY IN 1853, DOUGLAS is now chairman of the Senate Committee on Territories. Early last year, in 1854, he introduced the Kansas-Nebraska Act, which opened the vast northern portion of the old Louisiana Purchase, stretching from the Mississippi to the Rockies, to slavery. The act passed with help from Democratic president Franklin Pierce, over the furious opposition of antislavery congressmen in both parties. It disrupted the balance set by the 1820 Missouri Compromise, which had explicitly forbidden slavery in those territories—or anywhere north of latitude 36°30', roughly the country's north-south midpoint.

What was Douglas thinking? As always, he had his motives, spoken or unspoken:

★ The main justification he gave was "popular sovereignty," the right of people in each territory to decide questions like slavery for themselves.

★ He also claimed that putting slavery into the hands of each state would remove it as a federal issue, so different sections of the country wouldn't need to fight about it anymore.

★ Behind the scenes, he was using the act to win Southern approval for running the planned transcontinental railroad through Chicago, instead of points south.

★ He was probably trying to unite his party by removing slavery as a national issue.

★ He was <u>definitely</u> working to raise his own already-high profile.

Whatever Douglas's intentions, the law backfired badly. It drove abolitionists (those who wanted slavery abolished) up the wall without satisfying the slave states, it made slavery a *hotter* issue, it threw every party into disarray, and it made Douglas many enemies.

The Kansas-Nebraska Act is now speeding the disintegration of the Whig Party, which has been losing members to two new groups: the antislavery Republicans and the anti-immigration American Party. Some Northern Democrats are so horrified by the act that they, too, are joining the Republicans. You are not yet ready to desert the Whigs, but the act's passage still jolts you into reentering the political arena.

You criticize the act in a series of speeches around Illinois. You accuse Douglas of betraying the spirit of the Compromise of 1850, which established California as a free state and which he himself helped pass. You say his idea of popular sovereignty sounds nice but really doesn't apply to decisions about slavery: "When the white man governs himself, that is self-government; but when he governs *another* man, that is *more* than self-government—that is despotism."

You're also skeptical of his claim to neutrality on slavery. "This *declared* indifference, but as I must think, covert *real* zeal for the spread of slavery, I cannot but hate. I hate it because of the monstrous injustice of slavery itself. I hate it because it deprives our republican example of its just influence in the world—enables the enemies of free institutions, with plausibility, to taunt us as hypocrites."

DIDYA KNOW?

A despot is a ruler who hogs power and often uses it in cruel ways. Abe was comparing slave owners to tyrants like King George III, from whom America had won its freedom less than "four score" years before.

You actually blame Douglas more than you do the Southerners. "They are just what we would be in their situation." They didn't start slavery, only inherited it, and ending it is no simple matter. "I surely will not blame them for not doing what I should not know how to do myself."

Still, you are adamant that slavery must not spread. You know the Constitution tolerates slavery, but you've started reminding audiences about the country's *true* founding document, the Declaration of Independence, which in 1776 called it a "self-evident truth" that "all men are created equal." You argue that Douglas is ignoring that legacy: "Let no one be deceived. The spirit of seventy-six and the spirit of [the Act] are utter antagonisms. . . . Let us re-adopt the Declaration of Independence."

The Declaration has become a major theme for you and

will remain so. "When we were the political slaves of King George, and wanted to be free, we called the maxim that 'all men are created equal' a self-evident truth; but now when we have grown fat, and have lost the dread of being slaves ourselves, we have become so greedy to be *masters* that we call the same maxim a 'self-evident lie.'" It was an Indiana Democrat who called it that, which you consider un-American: "What would have happened if he had said it in old Independence Hall? The door-keeper would have taken him by the throat and stopped his rascally breath awhile, and then have hurled him into the street." Go, Abraham!

Your speeches around the state have roused opposition against the act—and won *you* many new fans. Some of them draft you to run for the Illinois Assembly again, and you win easily. But then you turn down the position, because holding it would disqualify you from something even bigger: the US Senate. (Senators in 1855 are chosen by state legislatures, not directly by voters, as in the future, and state legislators can't pick from among themselves.) Speaking and writing letters all over the state, you have now become a serious contender for the Senate, running as a Whig.

Your three opponents are all Democrats. One is the

En garde! Wait, where's my saber?

JAMES SHIELDS

incumbent, James Shields, with whom you fought that "duel" for Mary back in 1842.

Another is Governor Joel Matteson, and the third is your friend Lyman Trumbull. Shields favors the act, Trumbull opposes it, and Matteson has not made his position clear.

THE CHOICE

TODAY, FEBRUARY 8, THE HALL of the Illinois House of Representatives is packed as a hundred legislators gather to elect the state's next senator. They will keep voting, round after round, until one of the candidates gets fifty-one votes to win. Mary and her friend Julia Jayne (now Julia Trumbull) are both watching from the crowded gallery.

You lead the pack in the first ballot with forty-five votes, versus forty-one for Shields, five for Trumbull, and one for Matteson (some abstain). The Trumbull votes come from "anti-Nebraska" Democrats headed by Norman Judd of Chicago. Stephen Logan and Judge Davis, your two main advisors, are thrilled with the results, but in the following rounds you keep failing to achieve a majority, never rising above forty-seven votes.

As the voting drags on into the evening, you see that Shields's voters are starting to drift toward Matteson. Once it becomes clear that Shields cannot win, Judd's Democrats might in the end go for Matteson, or they might go for you. You suspect that a vote for Matteson means a vote for the act. You just don't know whether Judd's party loyalty will allow him to support a Whig, no matter how Judd feels about slavery. The Whig-Democrat rivalry just goes so far back. But here's the risk: if Matteson wins, slavery could expand its grip over the new American territories.

So those are the stakes. Now you're at six rounds—now seven, now eight—and Matteson is suddenly at forty-six votes to your twenty-seven, with Trumbull at eighteen. Do you hang in there and hope you win, throw your votes to Trumbull because he at least opposes the act, or get him or Judd to back you instead?

A. Hang in there and hope you win.

This is what Logan and Davis advise. They say your chances look good.

> Hang in there, Abe!

However, you can see that Matteson may have greater momentum. You'd like to win, sure, but it's also import-ant to you that the act's supporters lose. Winning the election could improve your political standing a great deal, but staying in the race contributes to the risk that Matteson could win.

B. Throw your votes to Trumbull.

You could tell your supporters to back Trumbull, so that the guy who started out with only five votes could actually end up winning. Trumbull and Judd would owe you big, and you'd certainly be demonstrating your devotion to the antislavery cause. But are you willing to sacrifice your own chance at victory?

C. Persuade Judd to back you.

Judd insists that his Democratic constituents would never tolerate his backing a Whig. Matteson, although a Democrat, has cleverly not announced his position on the act, which could give Judd the excuse he needs to switch to Matteson. There's even a rumor going around that Matteson is preparing to buy Judd's votes somehow. On the other hand, Judd *knows* you're against expanding slavery. Should you gamble on bringing him into your camp?

D. Persuade Trumbull to throw his votes to you.

This is the option that seems to make the most sense. You are ahead of Trumbull, so it seems right that you should be the candidate to continue in the race. But every round of voting is bringing Matteson closer to victory; do you have time to convince Trumbull to make the honorable choice? He has high political ambitions and may not want to sacrifice his own prospects.

THE REVEAL

YOU CHOSE ... **B. Throw your votes to Trumbull.** Here's what you care about: what choice is most likely to keep slavery from spreading? So you tell Logan to withdraw your name or "you will lose both Trumbull and myself and I think the cause in this case is to be preferred to men." Slavery is the defining issue of your time, and you will gladly sacrifice personal glory to stop its dire expansion. As so often happens in life, it is precisely that selfless decision that ends up *winning* you personal glory beyond measure.

In the end, you tell your supporters to back Trumbull, so the guy who started out with only five votes ends up winning with fifty-one in round ten. Logan actually weeps on the chamber floor, while Davis asserts angrily that "he never would have consented to the 47 men being controlled by the 5."

You take your loss with impressive calm; to you, your higher goal of containing slavery counts for more. "I regret my defeat moderately, but I am not nervous about it," you tell your backers. "On the whole, it is perhaps as well for our general cause that

Trumbull is elected." You even make an appearance at Trumbull's victory party to shake his hand.

THE AFTERMATH

NOT ONLY DO YOU IMPRESS everyone with your dedication to antislavery principle, but you also make major FOAs of both Trumbull and Judd. Trumbull soon writes that he will back you for Illinois's other Senate seat when Douglas comes up for reelection in 1858. Without Trumbull and Judd on your side, your future would look very different.

Perhaps Trumbull should have thrown his votes to you, but he's no Abraham Lincoln. Mary is so furious at him and his "two-faced" wife, her old friend Julia, that she stops speaking to them—for years.

Choice V—1858

Sizing Up the
LITTLE GIANT

THE CHALLENGE

YOU'VE ALREADY SACRIFICED *ONE* SENATE race to the cause of containing slavery. Now you have a second shot, but you're running for Senate against the toughest opponent you've ever faced. Just *how* honest should you be, Honest Abe, in your first big campaign speech?

THE BACKSTORY

YOU WERE SOMEWHAT DOWNCAST AFTER your loss to Trumbull, but Mary and the FOAs kept the faith. According to one friend, Mary "had the fire, will and ambition" to support you, insisting you "had no equal in the United States." The FOAs sometimes resented her involvement in your career, calling her "ambitious" (seen as unfitting for a woman), but you valued her advice. Seldom do you give a major speech without seeking her input.

Ironically, *she* is less open with *you* on household matters, often hiding just how much she is spending. In 1856, she sold some land (given by her dad) and used the money to enlarge your house, doubling the living area with a new east wing. When you next got back from the court circuit, you were so amazed by the changes that you jokingly asked a neighbor, "Stranger, do you know where Lincoln lives?" But the bigger house has proven helpful for your career, allowing you to host large meetings and parties.

GROWING PAINS

YOUR SONS HAVE GOTTEN BIGGER, too—and so has their mischief. William Herndon doesn't like it when you bring Willie and Tad to the office: "The boys were absolutely unrestrained in their amusement. If they pulled down all the books from the shelves, bent the points of all the pens, overturned the spittoon, it never disturbed the serenity of their father's good nature. I have felt many and many a time that I wanted to wring the necks of those little brats and pitch them out of the windows."

(FROM LEFT TO RIGHT)
1. LOCKWOOD TODD (MARY'S NEPHEW)
2. WILLIAM LINCOLN 3. TAD LINCOLN

Okay, then. Still you do not punish them, often saying, "Love is the chain whereby to bind a child to its parents." And the time you spend with them has not kept your legal business from growing, particularly in the railroad industry.

LEGAL HIGHS AND LOWS

ALWAYS FORWARD-THINKING, YOU'VE NOW handled about fifty cases for railroad companies, helping them spread the east-west connections that mesh with America's big north-south rivers.

Your most famous case, though, was not commercial but criminal. In May 1858 you defended Duff Armstrong, son of your New Salem friend Jack Armstrong, on a charge of murder. Duff was accused of bludgeoning a man to death. The main witness was 150 feet away but insisted he saw Duff clearly because of the moon overhead. You got the witness to repeat his story over and over, then blew him to bits by calling for an almanac. It showed that the moon had already set that night! Nice job, legal eagle. For old times' sake, you charged Duff nothing for saving his life.

Very astute, indeed.

By contrast, in 1855 you had your most humiliating legal experience ever, courtesy of Edwin Stanton, a brilliant but grouchy lawyer from Pittsburgh. Stanton and two fancy New York lawyers were representing a company accused of violating patents on the McCormick reaper, the market-leading machine for harvesting crops. Because the trial was set for Chicago, they needed Illinois counsel and hired you. You did a ton of careful preparation, only to see it ignored when the case got shifted to Cincinnati, Ohio.

You still showed up for the trial, but they treated you like an idiot, purely based on your looks and Western origins. "Why did you bring that damned long-armed ape here?" Stanton asked one of the New Yorkers. "[H]e does not know anything and can do you no good." Even though you all stayed at the same hotel, they completely snubbed you, not letting you join them for meals or utter a peep in court. You told Herndon you were "roughly handled by that man Stanton." If only Stanton knew what the future holds for you both!

A Storm Is Coming

YOUR LAW PRACTICE, BUSY THOUGH it keeps you, has not deafened you to the booming thunder of conflict over slavery. Boom: in 1855, thanks to the

Kansas-Nebraska Act (which lets each territory choose whether to allow slavery), guerrilla warfare broke out in Kansas between "Free-Staters" (who included both abolitionists and poor white farmers who didn't want to compete against slave-worked plantations) and "Border Ruffians" (immigrants from Southern states who wanted a proslavery vote).

We don't monkey around with military business.

FUN FACT

Not to be confused with feuding gorillas, guerrilla warfare means fighting a larger force through irregular attacks such as ambushes or raids. Guerrillas' speed and small numbers give them the element of surprise.

The country's leading newspaper editor, Horace Greeley of the *New York Tribune*, called it Bleeding Kansas and printed news of every ambush and massacre.

Boom: in 1856, abolitionist senator Charles Sumner electrified Congress with "The Crime against Kansas," a speech against Douglas and Senator Andrew

Butler of South Carolina, who was also involved in writing the Kansas-Nebraska Act. Sumner blamed them for the violence in Kansas, saying they were attempting to force an innocent territory into the evil embrace of slavery. His language was deemed so insulting to Butler's and South Carolina's honor that Butler's nephew, a representative, stalked onto the Senate floor with a heavy cane two days later and beat Sumner nearly to death. Sumner became a martyr in the North, while the nephew became a hero in the South.

Boom: in 1857, the Supreme Court, under Chief Justice Roger B. Taney, overturned decades of precedent with its infamous Dred Scott decision. Dred Scott, a slave, was suing for his liberty because his late master had taken him to Illinois and other free territories for several years. Taney (born to a slaveholding family of tobacco planters) ruled that Congress never *had* any right to outlaw slavery in any territory, so the Missouri Compromise and other barriers to slavery's expansion were actually unconstitutional. Scott was eventually freed by his new owners, but Taney's shortsighted decision made constructive dialogue over slavery almost impossible.

DRED SCOTT

In shock, you accused the Supreme Court of violating the spirit of the Declaration of Independence. Stephen Douglas disagreed and defended Taney, saying the signers of the Declaration must have (unless they were stupid or lying) "referred to the white race alone, and not to the African, when they declared men to have been created free and equal."

Democratic papers loved Douglas's speech; the *New York Herald* said it showed him to be presidential material.

Call and Response

YOU COULD NOT LET DOUGLAS go unanswered. Two weeks later, you explained that the Founders meant what they said: *all* people were created with equal rights. Obviously, slavery violated those rights in 1776, but they still intended equal treatment to be an ideal "familiar to all, and revered by all; constantly looked to, constantly labored for, and even though never perfectly attained, constantly approximated, and thereby constantly spreading and deepening its influence, and augmenting the happiness and value of life to all people of all colors everywhere." The Founders may have believed they could not pass the Constitution and abolish slavery at the same time, but that didn't mean they approved of slavery or wanted it to last forever.

In that speech on Dred Scott, you also addressed accusations from Douglas that you wanted black and white people to be treated equally in *every* way, even to the point of mingling and marrying. You tried striking a balance, which, sadly, reflected the bigotry of the era:

> *There is a natural disgust in the minds of nearly all white people,*

to the idea of an indiscriminate amalgamation of the white and black races, and Judge Douglas is [trying to get] the benefit of this disgust to himself. . . . Now I protest against that counterfeit logic which concludes that, because I do not want a black woman for a <u>slave</u>, I must necessarily want her for a <u>wife</u>. I need not have her for either, I can just leave her alone. In some respects she is certainly not my equal; but in her natural right to eat the bread she earns with her own hands without asking leave of anyone else, she is my equal, and the equal of all others.

You've been thinking a *lot* about Douglas since your loss to Trumbull. In late 1856, you jotted down these thoughts: "Twenty-two years ago Judge Douglas and I first became acquainted. Even then, we were both ambitious; I, perhaps, quite as much so as he. With *me,* the race of ambition has been a failure—a flat failure; with him it has been one of splendid success." But Douglas does not care about the "oppressed of my species," you implied, while your dearest hope is to help them rise with you. You believe the Kansas-Nebraska Act has made Douglas vulnerable, and you plan to stop him from getting reelected. Now that the Whig Party is pretty much finished, you will run as a Republican.

THE CHOICE

NOW THE **ILLINOIS REPUBLICANS ARE** meeting to choose a Senate candidate, and you are the likely nominee, partly because people remember your principled stand for Trumbull and against slavery, which cost you the last Senate election. To clinch the nomination, you've drafted a speech that begins with an attack on the act (and so on Douglas) but then goes much further:

We are now far into the _fifth_ year, since a policy was initiated, with the _avowed_ object, and _confident_ promise, of putting an end to slavery agitation. Under the operation of that policy, that agitation has not only, _not ceased_, but has constantly augmented. In my opinion, it _will_ not cease, until a _crisis_ shall have been reached, and passed. "A house divided against itself cannot stand." I believe this government cannot endure, permanently half _slave_ and half _free_. I do not expect the Union to be _dissolved_—I do not expect the house to _fall_—but I do expect it will cease to be divided. It will become _all_ one thing, or _all_ the other.

The draft goes on to explain that either slaveholders will agree to put slavery on a path to extinction, or they will succeed in getting slavery approved in _every_ state, but the current split within the country can't continue. This opening goes way beyond other speeches you've given; in a way, it implies that the act is just hastening the inevitable, because the compromises it scrapped were not real fixes, either.

Punchy, yes? But your friends hate this draft. They're worried it goes too far, seems too extreme, will scare conservative voters. It may be true, they caution, but telling that truth could lose you the election. They may be right; perhaps you should consider skipping the opening or toning it down, or saving the idea for later, when you plan to debate Douglas. Or you could ignore your friends, which you can't do too often if you want to keep their support.

What are you going to stand for, Abraham—and when?

WHAT DO YOU DO, ABRAHAM? SELECT ONE:

A. Never mention your "house divided" idea.

Mary tells you the "house divided" speech will make you president, and you think she might be right. The line comes from Scripture, but you're applying it in a bold new way. Here's why: you believe the country has to face up to the fact that slavery is *not* going away as an issue. Compromise hasn't worked. The Douglas notion of "popular sovereignty" obviously isn't working, as "Bleeding Kansas" shows. You believe nothing will work but to resolve this conflict, one way or the other. But should you show your cards now? Your reputation and Senate position are at stake. Should you delay speaking out until your political position is more secure?

B. Tone down the opening.

You could start off on a lighter note, particularly because the rest of the speech is pretty strong stuff. You call popular sovereignty "squatter sovereignty" and say that the "sacred right of self-government" is being "perverted" by Douglas to mean that "if any *one* man, choose to enslave *another*, no *third* man shall be allowed to object." You also accuse Douglas of being too wishy-washy. "How can he oppose the advances of slavery? He don't *care* anything about it."

However, the way a speech is introduced can make it less offensive to those who disagree. Maybe if you tone down the opening, the speech as a whole won't come off as extreme as the draft version does.

C. Say what you wrote.

The draft version may be too forceful for some, but you also feel it's got important thoughts for people to hear.

After all, this is the speech where you say Douglas may be a "great man," but call him "caged and toothless" when it comes to fighting slavery. And a battle over slavery is coming, make no mistake: you even accuse Justice Taney of laying the groundwork for a decision that slavery must be legalized in *free* states. "We shall *lie down* pleasantly dreaming that the people of *Missouri* are on the verge of making their State *free;* and we shall *awake* to the *reality,* instead, that the Supreme Court has made *Illinois* a *slave* State." The "house divided" opening adds oomph to your overall message, but is there such a thing as *too much* oomph?

D. Save the "house divided" idea for the debates.

You'll have plenty of other chances to speechify. Elections in the 1850s involve many one-on-one debates, often hours long. Perhaps it would be wiser to hold off on "house divided" until you've had more chances to assess the political climate, instead of using it to launch your whole campaign.

THE REVEAL

YOU CHOSE ... **C. Say what you wrote**. Which was a bold move. Years from now, you will say, "If I had to draw a pen across my record, and erase my whole life from sight, and I had one ... choice left of what I should save from the wreck, I should choose that speech and leave it to the world unerased."

THE AFTERMATH

YOUR SPEECH WINS YOU HUGE applause and the nomination but does scare some critics. They say you sound like an abolitionist, or that you're calling for civil war. Not at all, you explain to the papers: you just want slavery "fairly headed off" from new territories, so that it can die out naturally, without federal intervention, in the South. Overall, your argument works; your speech about *division* will serve to *unify* the Republican Party behind you.

Douglas invites you to hear *his* campaign kickoff speech a few weeks later. In it he defends Taney again: "This government of ours is founded on the white basis. It was made by the white man, for the benefit of the white man, to be administered by white men." Yikes! He goes on: you can't just "say that slavery is an evil and hence should not be tolerated. You must allow the people to decide for themselves whether it is a good or an evil." He says you're a troublemaker who's provoking "a war of sections, of the North against the South, of the free states against the slave states." This is going to be quite a campaign.

You challenge Douglas to debate in up to fifty towns all over Illinois so the voters can hear your differing views. As a famous incumbent he'd rather not share his audiences, but he can't look chicken, so eventually he agrees to the fewest debates he can, a mere seven. They take place from August through October, attracting tens of thousands, and you each give dozens of other speeches along the way.

Douglas travels in a deluxe private train bedecked with flags and a banner that reads STEPHEN A. DOUGLAS, THE CHAMPION OF POPULAR SOVEREIGNTY. His production values even include a cannon that fires to announce his arrival in each new town. (Seriously?) *You* travel by regular train or horse and wagon. Douglas rocks ruffled shirts and embroidered vests; *you* show up in rumpled, ill-fitting black suits.

Douglas's national fame attracts reporters from major newspapers, who become increasingly impressed—by his gangling opponent. Here's the *New York Evening Post:* "I must confess that long Abe's appearance is not comely [i.e., not handsome]. But stir him up and the fire of his genius plays on every feature. . . . You have before you a man of rare power and magnetic influence."

You become known for some great zingers from this period—some too good to forget, even if you may not actually have said them. This skeptical remark to Douglas, for example: "You can fool all the people some of the time, and some of the people all the time, but you cannot fool all the people all the time." Or, when Douglas calls *you* two-faced: "I leave it to my audience.

If I had another face, do you think I'd wear this one?"

You definitely accuse Douglas of using a "fantastic arrangement of words, by which a man can prove a horse chestnut to be a chestnut horse." Douglas spends much of his time calling you things like "Black Republican" (eighteen times in one debate!) and trying to scare voters with the idea that you love slaves: "I do not question Mr. Lincoln's conscientious belief that the negro was made his equal, and hence is his brother, but for my own part, I do not regard the negro as my equal, and positively deny that he is my brother or any kin to me whatever."

Given how racist Illinois is (its constitution actually prohibits free blacks from settling there!), you have to counter this hateful attack. That unfortunately means expressing the kind of bigotry most people expect in 1858: "I am not, nor ever have been, in favor of bringing about in any way the social or political equality of the white and black races . . . of making voters or jurors of negroes, nor of qualifying them to hold office, nor to intermarry with white people." You probably mean this all now, but your position will keep evolving toward equality over the coming years.

STOCKING YOUR CABINET

THE CHALLENGE

GOOD NEWS: THOUGH YOU LOST the Senate race to Douglas, you've won the race for president! Bad news: the country's at risk of a bloody civil war. You must select only the best for your cabinet—but what does "best" even mean in times like these?

THE BACKSTORY

GIVEN YOUR "MEMORABLE AND BRILLIANT" performance in the 1858 Senate campaign (thanks,

Chicago Tribune), it was only logical that you would win. But you, uh, didn't.

Senators, remember, are still picked by state legislators. You Republicans got more *votes* in the Illinois legislative election, but the voting districts had been cunningly arranged by Democrats (who had long controlled the state government) so that they won more *seats*. So the legislature sent Democrat Stephen Douglas back to Washington, while you stayed home. You told a friend, "I feel like the boy who stumped [stubbed] his toe. I am too big to cry and too badly hurt to laugh."

The Contenders

THERE WERE CONSOLATIONS, THOUGH. The *Tribune* was right in saying, "He has created for himself a national reputation which is both envied and deserved." Winning a popular majority (in a historically Democratic state) against Douglas, a man widely seen as the country's best politician, instantly made you a contender for the Republican presidential nomination.

The next month, Jesse Fell, secretary of the Illinois Republican Committee, asked you for some biographical info. Why? Because he wanted to promote you as the committee's favorite for president. You told him thanks but no thanks: "There is nothing in my early history that would interest you or anyone else." Besides, why should you stand in the way of better-known Republicans from out of state, such as William Seward and Salmon Chase?

Salmon Chase for president? Sounds a little fishy to me.

Seward, a former Whig, was the clear front-runner. Having served New York as governor and senator (twice each!), he also had decades of antislavery credentials. As governor in 1839, he refused to hand over three free black sailors to Virginia, which was demanding them because they'd helped a slave escape. As a senator in 1850, he opposed the Fugitive Slave Act, appealing in a famous speech to a "higher law" than the Constitution. And in 1858, he described an "irrepressible conflict" between the North and the South, which would continue until the slavery issue was resolved—a bit like your "house divided" speech, only more militant in tone. Seward's passionate speechifying was uplifting (one listener said he "would inspire a cow with statesmanship if she understood our language") but made him sound more radical than he actually was. That made some conservative Republicans reluctant to back him, but he had many more fans than critics.

Chase was even more adamantly against slavery than Seward. He defended so many escaped slaves in Northern courts that he was called the "attorney general for fugitive slaves." Like Seward, he served in the Senate and as a governor (for Ohio), but he left the Whigs well before Seward did, choosing to make slavery his main issue. His major weakness among Republicans was his free-trade stance: most of them favored a system of tariffs to protect US companies. But he was six foot two and handsome, a perfect statesman by appearance. All in all, another strong contender.

So you had good reason to be modest about your chances, once even admitting, "I must, in candor, say I do not think myself fit for the Presidency." On the other hand, you probably also sensed that there was nothing to be gained by throwing your hat in the ring too soon. Instead, you spent a year repairing your bank balance; you'd taken a break from law to campaign in 1858, and with all Mary's spending, you needed the money.

DIDYA KNOW?

Mary Todd Lincoln was minted on a US coin just like her husband. As a major shopper herself, she likely would've been pleased to know people could use her image to buy things!

LIFE OF THE PARTY

IN YOUR SPARE TIME, YOU helped coordinate Republicans around the country to shape the party's message—a task for which your debate experience and growing renown put you much in demand. To a Boston group you wrote that Democrats "hold the *liberty* of one man to be absolutely nothing, when in conflict with another man's right of *property*." To state party leaders you sent advice to avoid radical platform planks (about repealing the Fugitive Slave

Act, for instance) that might scare centrist voters. You accepted invitations to speak in five states (Indiana, Iowa, Kansas, Ohio, and Wisconsin) and rejected many others.

Last October, in 1859, came another thunderclap in the gathering storm over slavery. Boom: John Brown, an abolitionist already known for bloody encounters in Kansas, led a fatal raid against the US Army armory in Harpers Ferry, Virginia (today it's in West Virginia). He was trying to seize arms for a general slave uprising—which never materialized. Although he was soon captured—by Colonel Robert E. Lee—and executed, what really brought Southern tempers to a boil was that many in the North called John Brown a hero. You chose a more conciliatory approach, instead faulting Brown for "a crime against the state."

A WAY WITH WORDS

IN DECEMBER, YOUR DECISION TO stall on entering the presidential race paid off big-time. Advocates for each of the leading contenders (Seward, Chase, Edward Bates of Missouri, and Simon Cameron of

Pennsylvania) wanted the Republican nominating convention held in their candidate's home state. At the party meeting to organize the convention, FOA Norman Judd—the one who picked Trumbull over you for Senate—quietly suggested Illinois as "good neutral ground." Because no one saw you as a threat, Judd's town of Chicago ended up narrowly beating out St. Louis. As in real estate, location turned out to be crucial.

It was only after Judd succeeded that you finally sent Jesse Fell your biographical data. Even then, you didn't go for the hard sell: you sent a mere 606 words, with this unassuming note: "There is not much of it, for the reason, I suppose, that there is not much of me. If anything is to be made of it, I wish it to be modest, and not to go beyond the materials."

Your dark-horse campaign really started to gallop in February, when you won your first major newspaper endorsement (thanks again, *Chicago Tribune*!) and, more important, delivered a game-changing speech. That happened, ironically, in Seward's own state of New York, where you'd been invited by a Chase supporter who hoped you might take away enough Seward votes to let Chase slip ahead.

The speech was called the Cooper Union speech, after the college in Manhattan where you gave it. You prepared extra hard, knowing you'd be facing a crowd of big-city sophisticates, delivering your first speech on a national stage. No pressure! According to Herndon, "No former effort in the line of speech-making had cost Lincoln so much time and thought as this one."

It was worth it.

You built a strong case that the Constitution's framers intended the federal government to keep slavery out of all new territories. You called out the Southern states for threatening secession if they didn't get the president they wanted: "But you will not abide the election of a Republican President! In that supposed event, you say, you will destroy the Union; and then, you say, the great crime of having destroyed it will be upon us!"

For which you gave this telling analogy: "A highway-man holds a pistol to my ear, and mutters through his teeth, 'Stand and deliver, or I shall kill you, and then you will be a murderer!'"

You ended with this ringing call to action: "Neither let us be slandered from our duty by false accusations against us, nor frightened from it by menaces of destruction to the Government nor of dungeons to ourselves. LET US HAVE FAITH THAT RIGHT MAKES MIGHT, AND IN THAT FAITH, LET US, TO THE END, DARE TO DO OUR DUTY AS WE UNDERSTAND IT."

You got a huge standing ovation, raves from Horace Greeley's *New York Tribune* and many other papers, and immediate invitations to speak all over New England.

I tip my hat to you, Abe.

HORACE GREELEY

Before returning home, you went on to deliver similar speeches in Connecticut, Rhode Island, and New Hampshire. In one you added a masterful metaphor, which explained in simple terms why you opposed slavery's expansion:

> *If I saw a venomous snake crawling in the road, any man would say I might seize the nearest stick and kill it; but if I found that snake in bed with my children, that would be another question. I might hurt the children more than the snake, and it might bite them. . . . But if there was a bed newly made up, to which the children were to be taken, and it was proposed to take a batch of young snakes and put them there with them, I take it no man would say there was any question how I ought to decide!*

From that month on, you were a serious candidate for the Republican nomination. Still, you played it cool. "My name is new in the field; and I suppose I am not the *first* choice of a very great many," you told your team, planning how to approach convention delegates. "Our policy, then, is to give no offense to others—leave them in a mood to come to us, if they shall be compelled to give up their first love."

PULLING AHEAD

YOUR STRATEGY WORKED. WITH SEWARD the front-runner, the nomination was his to lose—and he did. Not only did some states think him too radical, but he also made a major error in refusing to campaign before the May convention, instead spending months touring Europe, meeting with heads of state as if he'd already been elected. The influential Greeley, once a major Seward fan, had also turned against him because of a personal grudge that Seward underestimated.

Au revoir, White House.

WILLIAM H. SEWARD

Salmon Chase was so sure *he* deserved the nomination that he barely campaigned, either. Republicans perceived him as "honestly believing that he owed it to the country and that the country owed it to him that he should be President." His vanity (he refused to wear glasses in public despite his poor eyesight, passing friends outside as if they were strangers) blinded him to all obstacles, including centrists' concerns about his radical abolition-ist stance. His rigidity (he never read novels and rarely laughed) and sense of entitlement had also made him enemies in his home state of Ohio, enemies who ended up casting the deciding votes for . . . you.

Edward Bates, a former congressman and Missouri attorney general, was Greeley's new favorite and was more conservative than Seward, Chase, or even you.

But he hadn't been active in politics for years, had once owned slaves, and had offended some immigrant Republicans because of a previous stint with the anti-immigrant American Party.

Finally, Senator Cameron never had much chance at the nomination, given his widespread reputation for taking bribes from railroads, banks, and anyone else who could pay. (He is credited with saying that "an honest politician is one who, when he is bought, stays bought.") Still, he had influence among the delegates from his state of Pennsylvania, so he could either assist or hurt you if he so chose.

WHAT FRIENDS ARE FOR

WITH ALL THOSE FACTORS IN play, here's how the FOAs helped you win the nomination. Judd, as the main host of the convention, put the New York and Pennsylvania delegations at opposite ends of the hall so that Seward's guys could not easily link with Cameron's. He also let Chicago crowds shove their way in at key moments, shouting your name. Davis pitched in by negotiating with the Bates and Cameron camps and in general running your Chicago operations. (The candidates themselves were not present, following tradition.) Many other FOAs, who'd moved to Illinois from other states, lobbied hometown friends to make you at least their second choice. You set the grand strategy, but in the end you got by with a *lot* of help from your friends.

The country was taken off guard by your nomination. Abraham *who*? About half the *Republican* papers printed your name as "Abram." As for the Dem papers, they were shocked at the news. The *New York Herald* called you "a fourth-rate lecturer, who cannot speak good grammar," whose speeches are "illiterate compositions . . . interlarded with coarse and clumsy jokes."

Now *your* party has started calling you the Rail-Splitter—harking back to your log cabin youth, when you earned money by splitting fence rails. In 1860 it's thought unseemly and a bit pushy for nominees to campaign around the country, but you're not a complete unknown: you've previously been to twenty-three states and spoken in seventeen.

DIDYA KNOW?

Elections in the 1860s were nothing like ours today, where it is commonplace for candidates to visit almost every state.

You're also allowed to distribute your thoughts through letters, pamphlets, and allies who speak on your behalf. The campaign office from which you manage this huge effort is a single room in the Illinois statehouse; your whole paid staff consists of a bright twenty-eight-year-old named John Nicolay.

Mary rises to the occasion as your campaign partner, entertaining the many visitors who parade through your home when they can't see you at the office. Reporters take a shine to her: your pals at the *New York Tribune* call her "amiable and accomplished . . . vivacious and graceful . . . a sparkling talker." She considers herself your main advisor, warning you away from people she doesn't trust, such as Judd and Trumbull. Maybe she even has something to do with the wagonloads of women who campaign for you with banners that read, WESTWARD THE STAR OF EMPIRE TAKES ITS WAY. WE LINK-ON TO LINCOLN, AS OUR MOTHERS DID TO CLAY.

FUN FACT

John George Nicolay would serve as Lincoln's secretary until his assassination, after which Nicolay and fellow secretary John Hay collaborated on a ten-volume Lincoln biography.

The Votes Are In

YOU FACE A SPLINTERED OPPOSITION in the general election: Southern Democrats nominate President Buchanan's vice president, John Breckinridge of Kentucky; Northern Dems nominate Douglas, who's too centrist for the South; and a few Whig and American Party holdouts team up as the Constitutional Union Party to nominate John Bell of Tennessee.

Douglas claims that he's the only one who can stave off civil war, and that you're determined to force full black equality on the slave states. Your speeches show no intention of interfering with slavery in the South, nor any belief that the president has a legal right to do so, nor any desire (yet) for full equality even in the North. But the Dems' newspapers don't print your speeches. In the end, with the electorate divided as it has not been before, you get less than 40 percent of the popular vote.

It's enough, though. Douglas scores below 30 percent and the others much lower, so you come out in first place. In electoral votes, which actually determine who goes to the White House, your victory is more lopsided. You win almost 60 percent, and Douglas not even 4 percent, because every Northern state ends up deciding for you.

Tonight, election night, you stay at the telegraph office until two; once your victory is assured, you rush home with the amazing news: "Mary! Mary! We are elected!"

THE CHOICE

MARY GOES TO BED REJOICING, but you have too much on your mind to sleep. Alone, you ponder one of the most important decisions a new president can make: whom to invite into your cabinet. "I then felt," you'll recall, "as I never had before, the responsibility that was upon me. I began at once to feel that I needed support, others to share with me the burden."

Carefully, you write eight names (including your own) on a bit of paper. Never one for self-importance, you place your own name *in* the list, not *above* it. You won't be showing anyone else this paper, yet with minor changes, the men you've listed will end up helping you in one of the greatest undertakings known to American history.

Do you choose FOAs, people you know and trust? If not, do you at least ensure consistency of opinion by picking people who share your moderate views? Do you go broader, including all wings of the Republican Party, to which you owe your victory? Or do you max out on inclusiveness, gathering Dems into your cabinet as well? Whatever choice you make will send the country a message, but you can't go just for symbolism. In these uncertain times, the people you choose for such key positions could help determine whether the country survives.

WHAT DO YOU DO, ABRAHAM? SELECT ONE:

A. Fill the cabinet with friends you know and trust.

You know your faithful FOAs would have your back. You've done favors for many of them, which they'd be happy to repay; they would certainly be willing to help you and support your positions. One major complication of this option is that the FOAs live mostly in Illinois, and the country is divided enough without your trying to govern it with a bunch of home-state cronies. Do the benefits of having trusted friends by your side outweigh the costs of focusing too much love on your own state?

B. Stock the cabinet with moderate Republicans.

Ideological look-alikes have appealed to James Buchanan and other presidents for their cabinets, but you've never been shy about forging your own path. Your campaign promised you'd govern with "justice and fairness to all," even to people who didn't want you nominated or elected. However, filling the cabinet with your ideological soul mates could give you the unified support you need in these tension-filled times.

C. Balance the cabinet among conservative, moderate, and radical Republicans.

You actually convinced Seward and Chase to campaign for you after you won the nomination. Now that your strategy of relying on rivals has paid off and gotten you elected, should you extend it into your presidency? If you reach out to every group within the party, from a variety of places in the country, it could pay off in broad party support. But is it too risky to rely on a cabinet that campaigned *against* you up until the hotly contested Republican convention?

D. Include Democrats along with Republicans.

While there is a great deal of variety within the Republican Party, including Democrats adds a whole new level. You and the Dems have deep ideological differences, and the two parties are at each other's throats. That being said, including a few Democrats would demonstrate your commitment to the country's unity and your openness to others' perspectives. But would any Democrat even want to work with you?

THE REVEAL

You chose ... **C. Balance the cabinet among conservative, moderate, and radical Republicans.** Not only do you reach out to every group within the Republican Party, but you also seek the *leaders* of those factions, guys with far more executive experience and lifetime successes than you. Instead of playing it safe with friends, you choose a majority of your cabinet from people who until recently were your political enemies—and could become so again. As you explain to the *Chicago Tribune:* "We needed the strongest men of the party in the Cabinet. . . . I had no right to deprive the country of their services."

THE AFTERMATH

IT HELPS THAT YOU KNOW how to appeal to your rivals' vanity. For example, you originally got Salmon Chase to campaign for you with a display of modesty: "Holding myself the humblest of all whose names were before the convention, I feel in especial need of the assistance of all."

In December you offer William Seward the prize cabinet position, secretary of state. He takes you for a naïve country lawyer, still believing you should never have been nominated over him, but that actually gives him *two* reasons to accept your offer. First, as he tells his wife, he has no choice if he wants to "save freedom and my country." Second, he thinks you're such a pushover that he'll end up running the government anyway.

Chase wanted to be secretary of state himself but ends up settling for secretary of the Treasury, for which he'll turn out to be well suited. Edward Bates readily

Being secretary of state doesn't mean being the White House receptionist. The secretary of state is one of the president's top foreign policy advisors and often negotiates major deals with other countries.

accepts the position of attorney general. Simon Cameron probably doesn't deserve to be secretary of war, but he does have executive experience, you do want someone from Pennsylvania, and he did end up throwing his delegates behind you in Chicago, so you give him the job. In the end, *all four* of your convention rivals end up in your cabinet.

There's only one Illinois name on your list, Norman Judd, and him you end up dropping—partly because he's from your state and partly because Mary, unlike you, holds grudges. She remembers all too well that he caused your loss to Trumbull in 1855.

You actually try to include a Democrat, but no Dems of any importance are interested. You even hope to attract Southerners to your cabinet, but the closest you can get is Bates and another "border state" lawyer, Montgomery Blair of Maryland. (The border states between North and South are Delaware, Kentucky, Maryland, and Missouri; all of them permit slavery.) Blair, your new postmaster general, actually represented Dred Scott before the Supreme Court. Unlike most of your cabinet, he also supported you in Chicago, as did the other two members: Gideon Welles of Connecticut (secretary of the navy) and Caleb Blood Smith of Indiana (secretary of the interior).

FYI, your vice president is not a cabinet member. He is Hannibal Hamlin of Maine, whom you don't even meet until three days *after* your election. Selected by the party and not by you, he will play almost no role in your administration, spending most of it in Maine, where he'll make himself useful by volunteering in the coast guard.

128 MEN ON A ROCK

THE CHALLENGE

YOU'VE SELECTED A CABINET TO help pull the voters together, but the country of which you've become president looks . . . smaller than before. Now you face your first major decision in office. Brave American soldiers are trapped in a fort off the coast of South Carolina. How can you save them without starting a war—or surrendering before the war even begins?

THE BACKSTORY

IFE WAS BUSY FOR A president-elect.

As you prepared for your March inauguration, you continued to work out of the same fifteen-by-twenty-five-foot room in the Illinois statehouse, with John Nicolay as your entire paid staff. You found time for lunch with Mary and the boys, but your office was flooded with visitors (mostly looking for jobs)

FUN FACT

"President-elect" is the term for a president who has been elected but is not yet sworn into office. James Buchanan—the only president who never married—was the sitting president until Lincoln was inaugurated on March 4, 1861.

from ten to twelve each morning. From three to five each afternoon, you received them in your home. Mary had mixed feelings about seeing her parlor jammed with strangers, especially when she overheard one ask another, "Is that the old woman?"

You charmed reporters with your down-to-earth manners, even this Democrat: "He is precisely the same man as before—open and generous in his personal communications with all who approach him."

You also started proving that you're open to popular input. Before the election Grace Bedell, eleven, wrote from Westfield, New York, to suggest you stop shaving: "You would look a great deal better for your face is so thin. All the ladies like whiskers and they would tease their husbands to vote for you and then you would be President." You won clean-shaven, but you decided Grace might still be right. You began a beard that's become a part of your popular image. BTW, it also makes you the first bearded president.

BEFORE   AFTER

So Long, Springfield

YOUR LAST DAYS IN ILLINOIS were filled with goodbyes. You visited your stepmom and took care of some unfinished business: ordering a tombstone for your dad's grave, which had lain unmarked for ten years. In Springfield you rented out your house, handed off your remaining legal cases, and spent time with your many local friends. You asked William Herndon to leave the old LINCOLN & HERNDON sign hanging outside the office you shared: "If I live I'm coming back some time, and then we'll go right on practicing law as if nothing had ever happened."

Although you didn't prepare a farewell speech, such a large crowd came to see you off at the station on February 11, 1861, that you felt you must say something from the heart:

My friends—No one, not in my situation, can appreciate my feeling of sadness at this parting. To this place, and the kindness of these people, I owe everything. Here I have lived a quarter of a century, and have passed from a young to an old man. Here my children have been born, and one is buried. I now leave, not knowing when, or whether ever, I may return, with a task before me greater than that which rested upon Washington. Without the assistance of that Divine Being, who ever attended him, I cannot succeed. With that assistance I cannot fail. Trusting in Him, who can go with me, and remain with you and be everywhere for good, let us confidently hope that all will yet be well. To His care commending you, as I hope in your prayers you will commend me, I bid you an affectionate farewell.

The Other President

ON THE VERY SAME DAY, another American boarded the train for *his* presidential inaugural. Jefferson Davis, until recently a US senator from Mississippi, would be leading the Confederate States of America. In that context, remarks you made along the way, trying to calm people down, instead seemed out of touch with reality: "I think that there is no occasion for any excitement. The crisis, as it is called, is altogether an artificial crisis." Dream on, Abraham.

When your train stopped in Westfield, New York, you made sure to find young Grace Bedell in the station crowd so that she could approve your new beard. In Philadelphia on February 22 (Washington's birthday), you helped raise the flag at Independence Hall, site of the Declaration's signing, and told the crowd, "I have never had a feeling politically that did not spring from the sentiments embodied in the Declaration of Independence. . . . I would rather

Onward, to my birthday cake!

GEORGE WASHINGTON

be assassinated on this spot than to surrender it."

Why the talk of assassination? Southern states were furious at your winning the election. Here's a typical reaction, from the *New Orleans Crescent:* "The Northern people, in electing Mr. Lincoln, have perpetrated a deliberate, cold-blooded insult and outrage on the people of the slaveholding states." Notice that phrase "the Northern people"? Almost makes it sound like a separate country, doesn't it?

Said the *Richmond Enquirer,* "This is a *declaration of war.*" And private citizens expressed even more rage: every day your mail carried death threats from anonymous Southerners. The night before your Philadelphia speech, railroad detective Allan Pinkerton warned of a plot to kill you in Baltimore, which you would have to cross in a carriage to get from one rail line to another. (Baltimore is in Maryland, where slavery was legal and many citizens wanted to secede.) So you snuck out of Philadelphia ahead of schedule, without your stove-pipe hat or entourage, accompanied only by Pinkerton and your large friend Ward Lamon, a lawyer who'd become your bodyguard. Traveling overnight in a private compartment, and crossing Baltimore under cover of darkness, you arrived in DC about 6 a.m.

Lamon, taking no chances, had stuffed his pockets with guns and knives. The only friend who greeted you at the station, an Illinois congressman, got punched by Pinkerton, who mistook him for an assassin. Once you reached your hotel, a note awaited you in your suite calling you a racist insult and marking you for death unless you resigned. Welcome to Washington, Abraham.

Constructing the Cabinet

THE NEXT PERSON YOU MET with was William Seward, about to become your secretary of state, to whom you gave a draft of your inaugural speech. He responded with seven pages (!) of notes, some of which you actually used.

Stephen Douglas came that afternoon to coordinate one last attempt at reconciliation with the South. He was by then a surprisingly helpful ally. Even in October, once it was clear you'd win the election, he told his secretary, "Mr. Lincoln is the next president. We must try to save the Union. I will go South." He saw for himself down there how intense the anti-North feelings were and soon began writing letters and speeches calling secession criminal and begging the slave states not to follow through on their threats.

President Buchanan, by contrast, was no help at all. Although from the free state of Pennsylvania, he'd always been soft on slavery.

Meanwhile, some federal officials actually tried to *assist* the likely rebellion. Buchanan's secretary of war, for instance, ordered munitions sent to South Carolina just before it seceded. Someone even ordered the navy's ships to faraway shores, apparently so that it would take the country longer to prepare a blockade of the slave states.

The most constructive member of Buchanan's cabinet was Edwin Stanton, the lawyer who "roughly handled" you that time in Cincinnati. As attorney general, he was appalled at secessionist betrayals within the government and so began reporting regularly to Seward out of loyalty to the Union. It sure wasn't out of loyalty to *you;* to Democrats he ridiculed you as "the original gorilla."

On March 3, with inauguration a day away, Seward pulled the stunt of withdrawing from your cabinet, probably trying to keep Salmon Chase (who'd been wavering) out. You called Seward's bluff, conceding nothing and urging him to change his mind, which of course he did. Meanwhile, you pinned down Chase by submitting his name to the Senate (with the rest of your cabinet list) for approval, so he unexpectedly found himself being congratulated by fellow senators, after which he couldn't really say no. Hmm, looks like you may not be *quite* the pushover they take you for.

THE CABINET AT WASHINGTON

DIFFICULT FIRST DAYS

SECURITY MEASURES PUT DC ON high alert for your inauguration. The army positioned sharpshooters on rooftops along your route. Mounted soldiers patrolled the streets, but you refused the enclosed carriage prepared for you. Even at the risk of your life, you wanted people to *see* their new president. It was customary for the outgoing president to ride with the incoming one, so Buchanan did, telling you how happy he was to be heading home.

The speaker's platform stood in front of the Capitol, whose wooden dome was in the middle of being rebuilt in iron.

Welcome to Washington, Mr. President.

Inauguration of Abraham Lincoln - March 4, 1861.

When you rose to speak, you realized there was no place to put your cane and stovepipe hat. Douglas, in a meaningful gesture of support, stepped forward, smiling, to hold them for you.

Your inaugural speech promised the Southern states once again that you had no plans to interfere with their slavery, but you *would* perform your duty of upholding the Constitution. You didn't recognize their right to secede, because the Union predates the Constitution and was made permanent by it: "No state, upon its own motion, can lawfully get out of the Union. . . . I trust this will not be regarded as a menace, but only as the declared purpose of the Union that it *will* constitutionally defend and maintain itself." If war did come, you told the South, *you* wouldn't be causing it.

Your last paragraph, recalling the revolution that united all Americans, would go down as one of history's most beautiful pleas for reconciliation. Although it did not prevent war, it *did* stake the Union's claim to the moral high ground:

> *I am loath to close. We are not enemies, but friends. We must not be enemies. Though passion may have strained, it must not break our bonds of affection. The mystic*

chords of memory, stretching from every battlefield, and patriot grave, to every living heart and hearth- stone, all over this broad land, will yet swell the chorus of the Union, when again touched, as surely they will be, by the better angels of our nature.

Now, as president, you listen for feedback on your first official speech. Most Northerners are glad it leaves the door open for peace, but the South (predictably) hates the way you reject secession. Even in the North you have critics; one of the harshest is Frederick Douglass, an escaped slave who has risen to become one of America's leading abolitionists. He knows personally the torments of slavery and wants them ended *now*. He calls your speech a "double-tongued document, capable of two constructions. . . . No man reading it could say whether Mr. Lincoln was for peace or war." The worst part, for Douglass, is your promise to leave slavery untouched in the slave states if they rejoin the Union: "The Republican President bends the knee to slavery as readily as any of his infamous predecessors."

You've started settling into the White House. Mary's first words as you walked in together: "It's mine, my very own!" She has already begun redecorating, which the White House badly needs. She's also hired a dressmaker, Elizabeth Keckley, who used to sew for the wife of Jefferson Davis. Keckley, born a slave but now a successful businesswoman, will become Mary's close confidante.

ELIZABETH KECKLEY

Your office on the second floor has a splendid view of the Washington Monument (still only partly built) and the Potomac River. You share it with your staff, which has now officially doubled—to two, John Nicolay and his friend John Hay. A mahogany desk, some chairs, a couple of horsehair sofas, a table around which the cabinet meets on

Tuesdays and Fridays: this is where the people's business gets done.

THE CHOICE

YOU START YOUR FIRST MORNING at work with a document that demands your decision—and it's a doozy. Major Robert Anderson, the commander of Fort Sumter, needs help. Sumter, one of the few US forts in the South not yet seized by seceded states, will run out of supplies in only six weeks: "We are in desperate need of provisions. If we are not resupplied soon, we will have to surrender."

The fort sits on a bleak man-made island in Charleston Harbor. Anderson transferred his troops there shortly after South Carolina seceded, figuring it would be easier to defend than the mainland fort where they'd been stationed. He has only small cannons—he is massively outgunned by Charleston's shore artillery—and 127 men, of whom 13 are musicians.

Seward wants you to surrender the fort, which is impossible to defend. If you send in armed forces *trying* to defend it, he insists, you'll be seen as starting a war. Your general in chief, Winfield Scott, estimates that a rescue expedition would require six to eight *months*. Scott is a hero of the War of 1812 *and* the Mexican War, though now age seventy-four and in poor health. Most of your cabinet sides with Seward; the exception is Montgomery Blair, your postmaster general, who says surrendering unless you absolutely must would be a terrible sign of weakness. Blair brings you his brother-in-law, a former navy officer, who has a plan he thinks might work to restock the fort in time.

You send Ward Lamon and other agents south to scout the situation, wanting more information, but you're running out of time. The incredible pressure

of this decision sends you to bed with a head-splitting migraine.

The experts are telling you the fort's a lost cause, not worth starting a war over, while Congress (like Blair) wants you to defend what belongs to the country. Trumbull, no longer quite so friendly as he was back in Illinois, speaks for an impatient Senate majority when he passes a resolution on March 28: "The true way to preserve the Union is to enforce the laws of the Union. . . . It is the duty of the President . . . to use all means in his power to hold and protect the public property of the United States." That night you do not sleep at all.

The next day, you make your decision. Now you, who've never really run any organization, are experiencing what it's like trying to run a *country*. You tell an officer, "If to be the head of Hell is as hard as what I have to undergo here, I could find it in my heart to pity Satan himself."

So what's your verdict: surrender, resupply, defend, or attack?

WHAT DO YOU DO, ABRAHAM? SELECT ONE:

A. Surrender Fort Sumter.

Seward and Scott are telling you the fort is as good as lost already, but are you even able to surrender—legally, politically, or diplomatically? Legally, your presidential oath requires you to "preserve, protect and defend" the Constitution—and you're sure secession violates the Constitution (so sure you'll often call the Confederacy "the so-called seceded states"). Politically, you doubled down in the inaugural address, pledging to "hold, occupy and possess the places belonging to the government." Diplomatically, you see no chance of peace even if you give up

the fort: Lamon and others you sent to Charleston tell you that all traces of Union loyalty are gone there.

B. Send supplies.

If you do this and no more, you could provoke the South into attacking. Then you can say you didn't start the war. But will this half measure satisfy the Republicans in Congress?

C. Mount a strong defense.

Sending in reinforcements would certainly signal that you don't want to lose an inch of federal territory. The defense would be challenging, of course. The fort is isolated. It was built to protect against an attack from the sea, not the land, so its main guns don't point toward shore. Also, your overall PR strategy is to depict the CSA (Confederate States of America) as the aggressor, so sending in new troops before the fort is even under fire would be "off message."

D. Invade Charleston.

This aggressive strategy would please your allies in Congress. There's a risk it could help the CSA attract its own allies, though. England and France rely on Southern cotton, so they might use a direct attack on the South as an excuse to jump into war against you.

As far back as your Independence Hall speech, you declared that "the Government will not use force unless force is used against it." Do you want to stray from that principle now?

THE REVEAL

YOU CHOSE . . . **B. Send supplies.** Later you'll say that all the troubles and anxieties of your life were nothing compared to the weeks before the fall of Fort Sumter. In the end, though, the agonizing is worth it: you made the brilliant tactical decision to resupply, and nothing more.

Up to the last minute, Seward insists that surrender would remove a source of friction with the South, and most of the cabinet still agrees. Seward is close to Winfield Scott, having advised him on a failed presidential bid in 1852, so he gets Scott to say that resupplying is not only dangerous but impossible. Seward is so confident of his influence over you that he rashly stakes his reputation on it. He tells Southern friends the fort will be surrendered soon, and even leaks that story to several newspapers.

He underestimates your independence of judgment. As you later explain to Congress, giving up the fort "would be utterly ruinous; . . . at home, it would discourage the friends of the Union, embolden its adversaries, and go far to insure to the latter a recognition abroad—that, in fact, it would be our national destruction consummated."

When you tell Seward you won't hand over the fort, he panics. Having painted himself into a corner, he's desperate to change your mind. On April 1, he sends you a memo that basically implies you're not fit to govern: "We are at the end of a month's administration and yet without a policy either domestic or foreign. . . . Either the President must do it himself . . . or . . . some member of his cabinet." Guess who he thinks would be the best person to make these tough decisions?

Calling _Abe_ unfit? Surely that memo was an April Fool's joke.

APRIL

1

You respond firmly, but rather calmly, given his in-your-face arrogance. There was an election, and you won! There can be only one person with the final say on policy: "if this must be done, *I* must do it." Seward gets the message, and does not try again to challenge your authority. Now that he understands you really *are* in charge, he will put pride aside to become your closest colleague—so close that other cabinet members will begin feeling just a tad jealous.

Your decision is a masterstroke, as events will prove.

THE AFTERMATH

ON APRIL 6, YOU HAVE Cameron send a message to South Carolina's governor (not to Davis, since you do not recognize the Confederacy). You are sending provisions, you say, but no additional troops or weapons—unless the Southerners try to block the shipment.

Nonviolent though your words are, Davis and his cabinet take them as a direct threat. On April 11, they tell Anderson to surrender, or else. He refuses. At four-thirty the next morning, they shoot a single cannonball over the fort, soon followed by massive bombardment from forty-three mortars and cannons along the shore. The war has begun—but *you* didn't start it.

Your convoy of ships reaches the harbor soon after the South begins attacking, just in time to see the fort take dozens of direct hits. Major Anderson doesn't even fire back until 7 a.m., and he holds out until noon the next day. At that point, once it's clear that resistance will only get his men killed, he finally surrenders and takes them (with the tattered Stars and Stripes) north on the relief fleet.

You haven't handed over the fort (the South *took* it), but you also haven't shattered the peace. Instead, you've chosen the perfect middle path to keep the moral high ground and unite the North behind you. The beginning of this war, thanks to you, will help determine its end.

Break the
CONSTITUTION—
to Protect It?

THE CHALLENGE

THE SOUTH MAY HAVE *STARTED* the war, but you still have to win it. To do that, your advisors are saying America's sacred freedoms are *so* important that sometimes you have to take them away. Wait, what?

THE BACKSTORY

THE SOUTH'S ATTACK ON FORT SUMTER has begun the Civil War, which will turn out to be longer and more brutal than either side expects.

Most Northerners, in the first flush of war fever, believe the fighting will be over quickly. Only eleven of the thirty-four states end up seceding, with a mere nine million of the country's thirty-one million people. The North has way more than its share of the country's factories, railroads, and warships. What could go wrong?

Here's what. The South's people, first of all, know Southern terrain far better than Union troops do. They are also fighting to defend their homes and their way of life (at least the white ones are). Their stronger motivation makes them fight fiercely and stay more unified. Whereas Northerners are split over why they're fighting (most say to protect the Union, but others say to abolish slavery) and how badly they need to win (or even what winning means), such issues are never in doubt down South.

Although the CSA can be cut off from the sea by your naval blockade, its geography helps it in other ways. The Confederacy spans over 750,000 square miles—about the size of Britain, France, Germany, Spain, and Italy combined. That's a lot of hostile territory for the Union to conquer and control. Moreover, it's harder to attack an area that size than to defend it: because the Confederate armies are *inside* the borders, their supply lines are shorter, and they can rush from one front to another faster than your troops, who have to take the long way around the perimeter.

Perhaps the South's biggest advantage, though, is its military leadership. Jefferson Davis himself graduated from the famous United States Military Academy at West Point, led a regiment with distinction against Mexico, and served as secretary of war under Franklin Pierce. Before secession, moreover, most of the US Army's senior officers hailed from the South.

Robert E. Lee is a prime example. Winfield Scott is not physically capable of remaining general in chief for long, so he recommends Lee for the post, calling him "the very best soldier I ever saw in the field." Just one problem: Lee's family goes back generations in the proud Southern state of Virginia, where his father was governor. When offered the top position, Lee gallantly replies, "I look upon secession as anarchy. If I owned the four millions of slaves in the South, I would sacrifice them all for the Union; but how can I draw my sword upon Virginia, my native state?" Soon after, he resigns and heads home, where he will put aside any qualms about secession and go all in for the CSA, skillfully commanding its main army.

ROBERT E. LEE

Sorry, Abe. Home is where the heart is.

The South has no shortage of excellent generals, while you get . . . the others. The need for troops, and for keeping unity in the fractious North, also forces you to appoint "political generals." These are men with little or no military experience who can somehow recruit lots of volunteers, or who get sponsored by powerful senators or governors. This patchwork of leaders hardly makes for a well-coordinated command: the "political generals" have never worked together before and often feel free to bypass or even ignore their superiors. Some work out okay (such as Benjamin Butler) or even better (Ulysses S. Grant), but most are duds.

One colorful example is Daniel Sickles, a New York politician notorious for shooting a man to death, then getting acquitted (with legal help from Edwin Stanton) with America's first-ever use of the temporary-insanity defense. Not the cleanest résumé, yet he raises regiment after regiment, so you won't regret making him a commander—until you do.

Watching Over Washington

YOUR IMMEDIATE PRIORITY, NOW THAT war has begun, is to defend the nation's capital. DC is surrounded by two states, of which one soon secedes (Virginia) and the other still may (Maryland). From your office, you can see Confederate flags flying in Virginia, just across the Potomac River. If the rebels capture Washington itself, the war could be lost within days of beginning.

Tad and Willie set up a "fort" on the White House roof, complete with nonworking rifles and a log painted like a cannon. But that's, uh, not enough. The navy commandeers boats to patrol the river, while soldiers and police barricade the streets and guard government buildings. Still, you badly need reinforcements.

The US Army is tiny (16,000 men, including Southerners), so you issue a proclamation two days after Fort Sumter's capture, calling for 75,000 men to join, mostly from state militias. Stephen Douglas, in patriotic solidarity, has visited you to advise that 200,000 would work even better.

Though Douglas opposed resupplying Fort Sumter, he knows the Union now has to pull together. He offers you his full support and tells a friend, "I've known Mr. Lincoln a longer time than you have, or than the country has; he'll come out right, and we will all stand by him." When you ask him to whip up Unionist loyalty in the Midwest, he goes willingly. Sadly, he dies there of typhoid fever.

CONVINCING CONGRESS

YOUR PROCLAMATION ALSO CALLS FOR a special session of Congress. Given election schedules, the soonest the session can start is July, so you symbolically schedule it to begin July 4. The Constitution says only Congress can *declare* war, but Congress won't be meeting for a couple of months, so you use the president's powers as commander in chief to *make* war—you call up troops, order ships and arms, order a naval blockade, etc. In July,

Congress will ratify all these actions as taken under your "war power," a phrase no president before you has used. It helps, politically, that the CSA fired first!

Most Northern states gladly send you soldiers from their militias, with Massachusetts first to respond. The border states, not so much. "Kentucky will furnish no troops for the wicked purpose of subduing her sister Southern States," says one governor. "Your requisition, in my judgment, is illegal, unconstitutional, and revolutionary in its object," blusters another, continuing, "Not one man will the state of Missouri furnish to carry on any such unholy crusade." It will take major effort just to keep these folks from joining the other side.

THE CHOICE

IN FACT, THE WAR'S FIRST fatalities occur in a border state *north* of you: Maryland. As Massachusetts troops pass through Baltimore to protect DC, they're attacked by rioting rebel sympathizers, with blood on both sides. City officials visit you, asking that you direct soldiers around Baltimore from now on, to avoid further violence. You can't reroute the rail lines overnight, though, so you respond with some annoyance: "Our men are not moles, and can't dig under the earth; they are not birds, and can't fly through the air. . . . Go home and tell your people that if they will not attack us, we will not attack them." Seems reasonable.

Luckily, clever Benjamin Butler finds a way to bring New York's regiments south via Annapolis instead of Baltimore. Maryland allows its secessionists to burn some bridges along the way, but Butler quickly rebuilds them. His success does not make the problem of traitors in Maryland go away, though: they're constantly cutting telegraph wires, ripping up tracks, stirring up resistance, and obstructing your war effort however they can. The state cannot (or will not) stop them, which makes them the army's problem.

That raises a new issue: the army is too busy to follow the "due process of law" guaranteed by the Constitution. For example, the habeas corpus rule says no one can be arrested without sufficient evidence.

General Scott asks you to suspend habeas corpus, arguing that events are moving too quickly for his officers to conduct regular, police-style investigations. If these spies and saboteurs are not arrested fast, who knows what damage they will do? On the other hand, aren't you sworn to "preserve, protect and defend" the Constitution? If you start ignoring civil liberties, what exactly are you protecting?

WHAT DO YOU DO, ABRAHAM? SELECT ONE:

A. Arrest suspects when you have evidence.

This seems like an appealing middle ground: fight saboteurs while respecting due process. But would it work? The army is not trained in police work, has other priorities, and might not have time to gather proper evidence—especially not in hostile parts of Maryland. If lack of evidence keeps the secessionists at large, they could cut Washington off from all communication with the North, and maybe even deliver the crucial state of Maryland to the Confederacy.

B. Arrest suspects, evidence or not.

This choice does not stick to due process and could give you an image of being power-mad, but you think it could be the only way to keep control of Maryland. How can you balance due process and your own image versus the risk of losing Maryland to the Confederacy?

C. Don't arrest suspects—just watch them.

That way, no one could accuse you of stomping on civil rights. But how about your presidential oath to preserve the Union? Not to mention the human rights being trampled daily by Southern slave owners. The question is, how much liberty can you put aside while defending freedom?

D. Don't arrest suspects—just shoot them.

The Constitution actually says, "Habeas Corpus shall not be suspended, unless when in Cases of Rebellion or Invasion the public Safety may require it." This "Case of Rebellion" qualifies, right?

That said, perhaps shooting suspects is a bit extreme. Your goal is to win the war while preserving whatever rights you can. The question is, where should you draw that line?

THE REVEAL

YOU CHOSE ... **B. Arrest suspects, evidence or not.** You decide you can't afford to respect habeas corpus in this emergency. As you later explain, habeas corpus is indeed very important, but not more important than the Union itself: "a life is never wisely given to save a limb."

DIDYA KNOW?

The president of the Confederacy, Jefferson Davis, also suspended habeas corpus on February 27, 1862.

JEFFERSON DAVIS

You authorize Scott to "arrest, and detain, without resort to the ordinary processes and forms of law, such individuals as he might deem dangerous to the public safety"—but only along the Maryland railway lines. Those arrested are jailed in US forts, not local prisons. You view this as a reasonable compromise, acting "very sparingly," as you put it to Congress, and they agree. Habeas corpus is a precious American right, but you rightly ask, "are all the laws, *but one,* to go unexecuted, and the government itself go to pieces, lest that one [law] be violated?"

THE AFTERMATH

YOU THINK YOUR DECISION IS the right one. But Chief Justice Roger Taney, the same genius who led the Supreme Court against Dred Scott, says the choice is not even yours to make. He interprets the Constitution to say that only Congress, not the president, can suspend habeas corpus. For that reason, he accuses you of attempting military dictatorship and orders you to release the first guy General Scott arrested. Never mind that Congress can't suspend *anything* if it's not even in session yet.

Unlike poor Dred Scott, though, *you* don't have to do what Taney says. As attorney general, Edward Bates advises you and the army to proceed under your authority as commander in chief. Later, Congress will in fact suspend habeas corpus nationwide, which pretty much puts the seal of approval on your limited emergency action.

You're a lawyer yourself, so you're very conscious of precedent. You try to use your war powers only when they are absolutely necessary. During the war, the army will arrest more than 10,000 people without clear evidence, which is no small thing, but you'll generally try to err on the side of civil liberties, even overruling your generals when you deem it necessary.

Your decision in Maryland will remain controversial long after this war. Still, you deserve some benefit of the doubt: America may never face a greater threat than you're fighting. Later presidents will trample more civil rights against less dangerous opponents, making you look good by comparison. Unfortunately, they will often use your example as justification.

FREE TO
WIN?

THE CHALLENGE

YOU'VE TAKEN SOME RIGHTS AWAY from your countrymen in order to protect their greater freedom. But what about the *slaves'* freedom? You do want to liberate them, but how? Which ones? And are the American people ready for such a radical move?

THE BACKSTORY

IT'S NOW JULY 1862, SO you've been living in the White House for more than a year. Mary, the first president's wife to be called First Lady, is having a tough time in that role. Washington's two main social sets are both freezing her out: the Northern ladies mostly see her as an uncouth frontier woman, while the (remaining) Southern ones dislike her antislavery politics.

Mary does not get credit (or seek publicity) for her good works, including many visits to wounded soldiers, where she spoon-feeds them, reads to them, and helps them write letters home. When her seamstress, Elizabeth Keckley, starts a relief agency for the many slaves escaping across enemy lines, Mary raises money and often goes to their encampments, delivering food and blankets. To you she explains, "The cause of humanity requires it."

Mary tries to stay involved in your policy discussions, but she and your cabinet do *not* get along. She's especially bothered by your closeness with William Seward, whom you enjoy visiting after dinner for warm and wide-ranging talks but whom she has never trusted since he competed with you for the Republican nomination. Your cabinet resents her attempts at involvement; even your secretaries, Hay and Nicolay, privately call her names like "hellcat" and "Her Satanic Majesty."

You still listen to Mary, though. One topic she feels

especially strongly about is the punishment your army gives to soldiers who fall short in alertness or courage. Last October, she heard that a twenty-one-year-old private was due to be executed for falling asleep on watch. Mary brought Tad into your office to beg, "Think if it was your own little boy who was just tired after fighting and marching all day!" You couldn't resist writing out a pardon, which you brought to the War Department yourself. When the clerk asked the reason, you just said it was "by request of the Lady President."

In truth, you don't generally need much persuading to show mercy. You know how important discipline is to a successful military, but you are notorious among your generals for taking any excuse you can to pardon men who run from battle or fall asleep on watch. "If Almighty God gives a man a cowardly pair of legs, how can he help their running away with him?" you say once. Another time, you reduce to hard labor some death sentences for cowardice, explaining, "It would frighten the poor devils

DIDYA KNOW?

Abraham Lincoln granted 343 pardons during his presidency, many to deserters.

too terribly, to shoot them."
You'll even "pardon" a turkey from being eaten at the Thanksgiving feast you yourself have proclaimed.

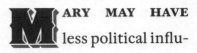

I hear eating turkey is fowl, anyway.

This Old White House

MARY MAY HAVE less political influence than she'd like, but she has gotten free rein in fixing up the White House. She quickly spent more than the annual allowance Congress gave for that purpose, requiring an embarrassing bailout. Many questioned her judgment, particularly with the country at war. You hated that when soldiers were not always getting the supplies they needed, she was splurging on "flub dubs for that damned old house."

Mary's image took another blow last year, when she saw a White House guest wearing a hat tied with purple ribbons. Mary had ordered a similar hat, but by then the shop had only *lavender* ribbons. As "Mrs. President" (a tag she's enjoyed using), Mary felt entitled to her choice of ribbon, so she pulled the other woman aside and made her trade ribbons.

MAMA'S BOYS

MARY'S WON NO POINTS FOR parenting skills, either. She (and you) let the boys burst into official meetings, keep a pet goat in the White House (it sleeps on Tad's bed), and harass cabinet members and other visitors. Please note: it's not polite to douse the secretary of war with a garden hose. Once Tad harnessed his goat to an overturned chair and rode it

like a sled through the East Room—in the middle of a formal party. Yelling, "Get out of the way, there!" to screaming ladies, he steered a full circle around the crowded room before heading out the back door.

Willie, tragically, came down with a mysterious fever in January, spending weeks in bed. Just when you thought he was getting better, he suffered a relapse. On February 20, hc dicd. You were heartbroken, murmuring, "My poor boy. He was too good for this earth."

Mary will never fully recover from the loss of your son. She spends days closeted in her room and nights weeping or holding séances in which she tries to contact Willie's spirit. She's not up to spending much time with Tad these days; without his brother and mother, he needs even more attention from you than before. (Two boys whom he and Willie used to play with are now banned from the White House; Mary says it "makes me feel worse to see them.") Sometimes Tad sits on your shoulder or knee during cabinet meetings. When you work late, he often falls asleep under your desk or next to the fire, and you carry him gently off to bed before turning in yourself.

Tad needs you, but you also cherish his company in these dark days of war and loss. Your many duties fill up every hour available, but even you must take breaks occasionally. You enjoy music, but strictly as a listener: you can't carry a tune or play an instrument. You love going to the theater when you can. You seldom focus on food: Mary sometimes has to remind you to eat, and even then your typical lunch might be just bread, milk, and an apple.

Don't forget your lunch, Abe!

But you like seeing others enjoy their meals—and one bonus of eating less is that it gives you more chances to entertain them with stories.

You still have an amazing way with a joke. One senator will call you "so funny he could make a cat laugh."

Lincoln's comedic timing was purr-fect.

How can that be, when your disposition has always been somewhat melancholy—and now that you've lost

Willie and have such huge responsibilities weighing on you? Maybe the seriousness of life as president gives you even more need to smile and joke when you can. As you once put it, "I laugh because I must not cry." Jokes for you are "the vents of my moods and gloom"; of course, you also use them for many other purposes, such as making a point, cheering others up, or changing the subject.

THE DIVIDED STATES OF AMERICA

JOKING ASIDE, THE STAKES OF your presidency could not be higher. If you cannot reunite the country, the USA and CSA might eventually split into even smaller pieces or be invaded by bigger, European powers. You believe that only a *United* States of America is big enough to guarantee democracy's survival in a world filled with monarchies.

If only your military efforts were going better. With General Scott ailing and in no condition to march, your general Irvin McDowell was completely outmaneuvered at the war's first major battle (Bull Run), and it's been downhill since then. You replaced McDowell with George McClellan, who was only thirty-four but had won a few minor battles in western Virginia, paving the way for Union sympathizers there to secede *from Virginia* and form the Union state of West Virginia.

Welcome to the Union, West Virginia!

McClellan *looked* like a gallant leader and was beloved by his troops, so you had high hopes for him. His biggest fan by far, though, was himself. "I find myself in a new and strange position here—President, Cabinet, General Scott & all deferring to me—by some strange operation I seem to have become *the* power of the land," he wrote to his wife after getting the promotion. "It is an immense task that I have on my hands, but I believe I can accomplish it." He has since proven to be one of the most effective generals of all time—for the *enemy*.

In the year since his appointment, Little Mac (as the troops call him) has shown all the daring and dynamism of an extremely stylish tortoise. McClellan exhibits amazing talent for bravado—every speech resounds with confidence, every report promises success—yet he always finds reasons *not* to attack. The men aren't ready, their supplies are low, the horses are tired, or (his favorite) he's outnumbered. He constantly overestimates the number of opposing troops (often doubling it) and is known for mistaking their desperately painted logs for cannon (seriously). By dithering and dallying, he's allowed Lee to continue building *his* army and fortifications between battles, so the Union controls no more of Virginia than it did a year ago.

McClellan never admits that anything is his fault—not even to himself. In arrogance, at least, he never fails: he often keeps you waiting, sometimes for hours, when you visit his HQ. In letters home, he calls you "an idiot" and "nothing more than a well-meaning baboon." Like so many conceited people, he hugely underestimates you: "I found the 'original gorilla' about as intelligent as ever. What a specimen to be at the head of our affairs now!" McClellan also happens to be a Democrat, pro-slavery, and personal friends with many Confederate generals; no wonder rumors abound that he is secretly in league with them.

You can see his failings clearly, but you haven't yet

found better talent elsewhere. When a senator demands that you replace McClellan immediately, you ask with whom. "Anybody!" he says, to which you reasonably reply, "*Anybody* will do for you, but not for me. I must have *somebody*."

FOLLOW THE NEW LEADER

ONE CANDIDATE SHOWING EARLY PROMISE is Grant, whose attacks on two forts in Kentucky were so overwhelming that the enemy surrendered without negotiation, earning him the nickname Unconditional Surrender (instead of Ulysses S.) Grant. Despite his sketchy background (bottom of his West Point class, expelled from the army for drunkenness, failed in every business he tried), Grant is beginning to emerge as your best commander—which, sadly, isn't saying much.

Here are my terms: we win, you lose.

ULYSSES S. GRANT

To supervise your generals and overcome their weaknesses, you need to understand military strategy. And so you've spent the last year doing something no one does better: soaking up huge amounts of information. You pore over tactical manuals, studying army theory and practice—ancient and modern, American and European. You often hang out at the War Department, writing orders to your generals, and you even visit them at the front—no fewer than eleven times during the war. Nicolay will remember, "He held long conferences with eminent generals and admirals, and astonished them by the extent of his special knowledge." As with anything else you undertake, Abraham, if you're going to be commander in chief, you're determined to do the best job you can.

Simon Cameron was no help to you as secretary of war, turning out to be as incompetent as he was corrupt. (A congressman from Cameron's home state of Pennsylvania once told you that he didn't *quite* think Cameron would steal a red-hot stove.) Cameron may have helped you win the Republican nomination, but he was your worst cabinet member, so in January you sent him off as minister to Russia.

You replaced Cameron with none other than Edwin Stanton—that same Stanton who had served President Buchanan as attorney general and once humiliated you in Cincinnati. Chase and Seward both insisted he was the man for the job, and they so seldom agree, that you took them seriously. In any case, Stanton proves to be perfect for the job: honest, smart, diligent, and so quick to anger that he makes a perfect "bad cop" to your "good cop" when handling headstrong generals and politicians.

Stanton is also effective because he doesn't kowtow to anyone—not even you. Once, you send a congressman to Stanton, along with a note asking Stanton to do the guy a certain favor. The congressman returns, spluttering that Stanton not only refused but called you a "damned fool" to boot. You show how secure you are by laughing it off. "If Stanton said I was a damned fool," you tell the shocked congressman, "then I must be one, for he is nearly always right, and generally says what he means." Over time, Stanton develops huge respect and affection for you, writing to his old law colleague that "no men were ever so deceived as we at Cincinnati."

Revenge of the Nerds

STANTON SHARES YOUR ENTHUSIASM FOR new military technologies. You've always been kind of a techie, with your patent filing and your belief in rationality, railroads, and infrastructure projects. Now you welcome inventors of new weapons such as machine guns and even newfangled ironclad ships—which pays off when your ironclad warship *Monitor* fights the South's larger *Merrimack* to a standstill in March, thanks to its greater agility and rotating gun turrets.

Meanwhile, you've got a country to run. You're dealing with Congress, the states, interest groups, other countries—and, most important to you, the American public. You take time for almost all the people who come to see you. You even host open receptions, which you call your "public-opinion baths," to keep in touch with what ordinary citizens are thinking and feeling.

You devote special attention to the four border states. Their slaveholders are one reason you don't position the war as a fight against slavery; you really, really don't want more states joining the Confederacy.

Delaware seems secure, given its location and politics, but Maryland could go either way. You cleverly allowed Union volunteers from Maryland to go home to vote last November, helping to elect a Unionist governor. As for Kentucky, its central location makes it crucial. You even reportedly said, "I hope to have God on my side, but I must have Kentucky." You were born there—but so was Jefferson Davis. The Kentucky legislature declared a neutral stance, which you were smart enough to respect: no recruiting in or marching through the state. Eventually, you maneuvered the South into attacking Kentucky first, allowing you to wear the white hat when you sent Grant to defend it.

Kentucky will spend the war on your side.

Missouri is the trickiest of the four states, partly because you made the mistake of sending John C. Frémont (former hero of California) to head the army in that area. He set himself up in a posh St. Louis mansion, surrounded by Hungarian and Italian guards in flashy uniforms; alienated the local politicians; lost track of the army's local cash deposits; and then declared martial law, putting himself above the state's government.

Thanks for the job, Abe! I will now ignore everything you say.

JOHN C. FRÉMONT

To cap it all off, Frémont decided to proclaim all Missouri slaves free! (Perhaps for political reasons: he had another run for the White House in his future.) You immediately overruled him, for three main reasons: no mere general could do something like that without consulting you; you didn't think he had the legal right; and his move could have cost you Maryland, Kentucky, and even support for the war among Democrats. Soon you replaced Frémont altogether, and Missouri has been calmer since then.

THE CHOICE

FRÉMONT'S HASTY ACTION IS FAR from the only way in which slavery has complicated your war effort. You keep stressing that secession, not slavery, caused the war; yet many of your friends and enemies alike can't believe that. Abolitionists can't imagine why *else* you'd be fighting, while many Northern Democrats (believing that the *Union* is the only just cause) suspect you of hiding your real motives. And the Southern (and border) states are convinced you're an abolitionist at heart.

Charles Sumner, the abolitionist senator, presses you to just do it: declare the slaves free already. You explain that the country is not ready for such a drastic move, though one day soon it may be. Last December you told him, "Mr. Sumner, the only difference between you and me on this subject is a difference of a month or six weeks in time."

Meanwhile, the war *has* been chipping away at Southern slavery, almost as if by accident. The process began last May, when General Butler was commanding a fort in the Union-controlled part of Virginia. Three slaves escaped from their owner (a Confederate colonel) to Butler, who then refused to hand them back. Butler was a proslavery Democrat, ironically enough, but he was also a clever Massachusetts lawyer who liked to say that he was a friend of Southern rights but an enemy of Southern wrongs.

Butler wanted to win the war. He coolly informed the outraged colonel that Virginia's secession made the Fugitive Slave Act void, so runaways no longer had to be returned. The colonel insisted that the slaves were still his property; if so, Butler countered, they were "contraband" (illegal goods), because the colonel had been using them for war purposes (building Confederate fortifications). The Union army was thus within its rights to "confiscate" the slaves and keep them.

You approved Butler's judgment, which then set a pattern for other Union generals to take and free slaves who were being used in the CSA's war effort. Three months later, Congress followed suit with its

Confiscation Act, which allowed the army to confiscate any Confederate "property" being used in the war.
Everyone knew that "property" included slaves, but the
act never mentioned that. In your December message,
you dropped in a reference to slaves "thus liberated,"
getting people used to the idea that confiscated slaves
were now *free*.

Now, in July 1862, Congress has passed the Second
Confiscation Act, which allows the army to seize *all*
slaves belonging to Confederate officials and soldiers.
The slaves already freed are proving a valuable source
of manpower (digging ditches, delivering supplies)
and information (about their ex-masters' locations
and troop movements). You've also started allowing them to serve in the Union navy—but not in the
army, where they might pass through sensitive border
states.

So how about it, Abraham? Is now the time to declare
all slaves free, even if their owners have nothing to do
with the CSA's government or army? The abolitionists
are growing impatient: not only is the war progress-
ing slowly, but millions are still cruelly and unjustly
enslaved. It's already a *year* since Frederick Douglass
wrote, "Let the war cry be down with treason, and

down with slavery, the cause of treason!"

On the other hand, plenty of voters in the North still oppose emancipation, as slave liberation is sometimes called. Even some Republicans, who join you in opposing the spread of slavery, do so mainly because they do not want black people in their states. And General McClellan, a Democrat, has recently handed you a letter warning you not to make this a war against slavery, because many in the army (including McClellan himself) will not fight for such a cause. (Way to be a team player, Little Mac!)

You've always been careful not to move too far ahead of public opinion. You'd rather bring it along with you, an inch at a time if necessary. In May, when General David Hunter issued an order freeing all slaves in the Southern coastal areas he controlled, you canceled it immediately. (Apart from bad timing, you objected to anyone's taking such major action without your permission.) As the war wears on, though, you can feel opinion shifting gradually toward emancipation. Should you perhaps free just *some* slaves, either where you can (in areas the Union already controls) or where your adversaries live (in CSA territory)? Or is it still too early to go even that far?

A. Free no more slaves for now.

This would be the cautious option, although your first instinct is to move immediately. Despite McClellan's letter, you think enough Americans are ready to accept emancipation. You've been watching public opinion carefully (you read about twenty newspapers regularly!), hiding your true feelings until the right time. As you said back in 1858, "[P]ublic sentiment is everything. With public sentiment, nothing can fail; without it nothing can succeed." To you, the time seems about right. But is it?

B. Free the slaves in areas you control.

Many abolitionists call this an obvious move. Slavery is evil. Even before taking office, you wrote to one Southern congressman, "You think slavery is *right* and ought to be extended; while we think it is *wrong* and ought to be restricted." Now that the country is at war over slavery, why settle for restricting it? Why not end it wherever you can, as soon as you can?

On the other hand, the border states might well secede if you try to free their slaves; they won't even let you *buy* their slaves. Also, you still believe you can't legally interfere where slavery already exists, *unless* it's to win the war. Would freeing the border states' slaves help or hurt the war effort?

C. Free the slaves in areas you don't control.

You like this idea. As you tell the cabinet, freeing the Confederates' slaves would "strike at the heart of the rebellion." Senator Sumner has pointed out that freeing the CSA's slaves could help win the war. First, you would win Europe's sympathies, ensuring that England and France stay out of this conflict. More important, the Confederate army could then be surrounded: as Sumner puts it, "You need more men, not only at the North, but at the South, in the rear of the rebels. You need the slaves." He has a point. Democrats and Confederates would mock you for liberating only those *outside* your power, but they're missing the point: you'd be doing it mostly to win the war.

D. Free all American slaves.

The border states might object, and there's the pesky issue of your constitutional power to free slaves in states that never seceded. But isn't slavery the root cause of this conflict? Maybe it's time to tear out that root once and for all.

THE REVEAL

YOU CHOSE ... A. **Free no more slaves for now.**
You conclude that the moment isn't right, mainly
because your army hasn't won many battles lately. For
the time being, you free no slaves.

Here's how it happens. On July 13, you confide a
preliminary decision (announce emancipation in the
South now) to William Seward and Gideon Welles,
explaining that "we must free the slaves or be ourselves
subdued." Nine days later, you read the cabinet a draft
of the Emancipation Proclamation.

But Seward convinces you it is still too soon: the war
has been going so badly that freeing the South's slaves
now might smell of desperation. You agree to wait until
the Union wins a major battle before issuing your proclamation. Little do you imagine how long that will take.

THE AFTERMATH

AUGUST 1862 DOES NOT PROVIDE you with the
kind of battle win that you believe would allow
you to announce emancipation the right way, so you
use that month to keep laying the political groundwork.

When Horace Greeley of the *New York Tribune* writes an editorial calling you "strangely and disastrously remiss" in not liberating the slaves already, you send him a widely reprinted letter stating your *"personal* wish that all men everywhere could be free." As *president,* though, "My paramount object in this struggle *is* to save the Union, and is *not* either to save or to destroy slavery." You're giving the reason for your proclamation *before* you announce it: "What I do about slavery, and the colored race, I do because I believe it helps to save the Union."

For that reason, your proclamation will allow freed slaves to serve in the Union army, a change you think will frighten the enemy. As Frederick Douglass has vividly put it, "We are striking the guilty rebels with our soft, white hand, when we should be striking with the iron hand of the black man, which we keep chained behind us."

But you can't issue the proclamation until your army wins a battle; well into September 1862, that still does not happen! Your squabbling generals lose the *Second* Battle of Bull Run. Attorney General Bates will write that you "seemed wrung by the bitterest anguish—said he felt almost ready to hang himself."

Then Confederate general Lee, knowing that a long war would favor the North, tries to strike a death blow by invading Maryland, hoping to curve around and take DC. You see his vulnerability while he marches as an opportunity, and direct McClellan to attack. Amazingly, he does! (It helps that a careless CSA messenger left Lee's secret battle plan in a field beforehand, wrapped around three cigars, so the Union knows his plans.) The Battle of Antietam sees nearly 23,000 men killed or wounded, making September 17 the bloodiest day of the whole war (and bloodier for Americans than the *whole* War of 1812).

McClellan loses somewhat more men than Lee, but Lee has fewer to spare, and his attack plans are ruined. Although McClellan lets *full* victory slip away by not sending enough of his troops into battle, and by allowing Lee to escape back into Virginia, Antietam still gives you the win you've been waiting for: on September 22, you finally issue your Emancipation Proclamation.

Even then, your announcement is only that: the proclamation will not actually go into effect until January 1, giving people even more time to wrap their minds around the idea. You will later tell a friend that going public earlier could have doomed the proclamation. Your metaphor is typical: "A man watches his pear tree day after day, impatient for the ripening of the fruit. Let him attempt to *force* the process, and he may spoil both fruit and tree. But let him patiently *wait*, and the ripe pear at length falls into his lap!"

The ultimate effect of the Emancipation Proclamation *will* be freedom for all slaves: not only does the proclamation help you win the war, but it also gradually helps the American people realize that slavery cannot be allowed to keep its foothold *outside* the Confederacy, either.

The word "gradually" may be an understatement. It will take years before slavery is officially abolished. Even the more limited Emancipation Proclamation ignites huge controversy when you announce it. The abolitionists, of course, think it does too little, with its limited scope and three-month delay. They want nothing less than a constitutional amendment forever outlawing slavery—which you know is out of reach for now.

The Democrats, on the other hand, accuse you of acting like a dictator. They call your "war powers" argument outrageous, a criticism convincing enough to win them many state and congressional elections in November 1862, though still not enough for a majority in the House or Senate.

Given the Republicans' poor election results, many people think you will not actually sign the official proclamation on January 1. But you refuse to go back on your commitment to the slaves, telling your advisors, "My word is out to these people, and I can't take it back."

Frederick Douglass, for one, says you "may be slow" but "will take no step backward. . . . If he has taught us to confide in nothing else, he has taught us to confide in his word."

In the meantime, you finally emancipate *yourself* from the burden of General McClellan, who went into such paralysis after Antietam that you complained he "has got the 'slows.'" Once the election season is over, you don't mind so much offending his many Democratic friends. (McClellan was all huffy even *before* you fired him, writing to his wife, "The good of the country requires me to submit to all of this from men whom I know to be greatly my inferior socially, intellectually & morally! There never was a truer epithet applied to a certain individual than that of the 'Gorilla.'" Any guess who he meant?)

On January 1, you stand for three hours on the receiving line at the White House New Year's Day reception, shaking hands. By the time you come upstairs to sign the formal proclamation, your own hand is sore and swollen. It starts to tremble as you sign with your golden pen, so you slow down to steady it, saying when done, "I never, in my life, felt more certain that I was doing right, than I do in signing this paper."

Thanks to your proclamation, about three million people are legally free, and over 180,000 blacks will join the Union army over the next two years. Even more important, your golden pen has produced a major turning point in the war: from now on, the army will be openly fighting for the cause of freedom.

Choice X—1865

THE
BITTER
END?

THE CHALLENGE

YOUR EMANCIPATION PROCLAMATION HELPED turn the tide against the South. After many hard-fought battles, you're now far ahead in the war, but that doesn't help the many soldiers who are still dying. Do you negotiate a truce or let the bloodshed continue? And how will you punish the rebels once the war's over?

THE BACKSTORY

I T'S MARCH 1865, FOUR YEARS since you took office, but you seem to have aged much more, Abraham. The cares of government and war have worn deep lines in your face, and your weight has dropped from about 180 to 160 pounds. In your secretary Hay's words, "He was in mind, body, and nerves a very different man from the one who had taken the oath in 1861. He continued always the same kind, genial, and cordial spirit he had been at first; but the boisterous laughter became less frequent year by year; the eye grew veiled by constant meditation on momentous subjects; the air of reserve and detachment from his surroundings increased."

No wonder. Since you signed the Emancipation Proclamation in January 1863, your life has been filled with conflict—and not just between North and South! You, Abraham, have been facing problems on *all* sides full-time, including with:

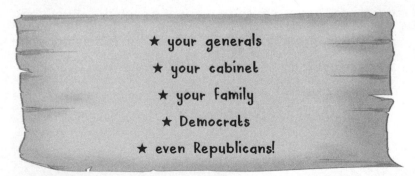

★ your generals
★ your cabinet
★ your family
★ Democrats
★ even Republicans!

Your generals. Having already dumped Generals Scott, McDowell, Frémont, and McClellan, you went through so many *more* commanders in 1863 that one cartoonist compared you to a fickle-minded kid constantly needing new toys.

You replaced McClellan with Ambrose Burnside, whom history will remember mostly for his bizarre facial hair (sideburns are named after him). He modestly turned down the promotion at first, saying he was "not fit to command an entire army." Unfortunately, he eventually accepted and proved himself correct. His reckless attack on Lee's army at Fredericksburg, Virginia, produced one of the North's worst losses ever; you accepted his resignation in January.

Man, I hate it when I'm right.

AMBROSE BURNSIDE

Next up: Joseph Hooker, called Fighting Joe for his aggressiveness. You appointed him, even though he'd reportedly said the war might be going better if led by a dictator instead of by you. Treasonous talk! But you didn't care much what he said if he could just win a few battles, calmly informing him, "Only those generals who gain successes, can set up dictators. What I ask of you is military success, and I will risk the dictatorship."

JOSEPH HOOKER

Fighting Joe was certainly self-confident, writing, "My plans are perfect, and when I start to carry them out, may God have mercy on General Lee, for I shall have none." But at Chancellorsville, Virginia, Lee scored what many consider his most brilliant victory, demolishing Hooker despite being outnumbered more than two to one. A visitor of yours had this impression when you heard the news: "Never, as long as I knew him, did he seem so broken, so dispirited, and so ghost-like. Clasping his hands behind his back, he walked up and down the room, saying, 'My God! My God! What will the country say? What will the country say?'"

In June 1863, Lee launched another northward invasion, this time all the way into Pennsylvania. You replaced Hooker with George Meade, known as the Old Snapping Turtle because of his grumpy manner with reporters.

Pardon, good sir, but I daresay we turtles have impeccable manners.

You figured Meade, a Pennsylvania native, would at least "fight well on his own dunghill," defending his home state. Once again, you saw the weakness in Lee's exposed position; you called it "the best opportunity we have had since the war began."

The next day, July 1, proved you correct. The two sides, with 165,000 troops in total, met at the small town of Gettysburg. Over three bloody days of fighting, Meade won the battle, partly thanks to CSA errors. (The North made mistakes, too. Remember Dan Sickles, the "political general" who was acquitted of murder on the grounds of temporary insanity? He ignored Meade's orders and got most of his own corps smashed in the battle, also losing his leg to a cannonball. He donated the leg to the Army Medical Museum, saying he would visit it once a year.)

At Gettysburg, the Union once again missed a chance to destroy Lee's forces, which you saw as the top priority. You sent Meade a telegraph saying DO NOT LET THE ENEMY ESCAPE, and what did he do? He let Lee and his men escape into Virginia. You could not contain your frustration, telling your secretary Hay: "We had them within our grasp. We had only to stretch forth our hands and they were ours."

GRANT AT LAST

GOODBYE, MEADE. IN EARLY 1864, you finally put Ulysses Grant in charge. After a long and brutal siege, Grant captured Vicksburg, Mississippi, which controlled the Mississippi River. Combined with

Gettysburg, this victory meant the war was finally heading in your favor. When his critics brought you rumors that Grant drank to excess, you said you just wanted to know what brand of whiskey he drank so that you could send a barrel to your other generals.

Grant soon proved he was a far better general for this war than George McClellan:

★ McClellan based his headquarters in a ritzy mansion near the White House, but Grant avoided DC's distractions by operating from the field.

★ McClellan focused on attacking the CSA capital of Richmond, Virginia, but Grant understood that the enemy forces were a more important target. "Lee's army will be your objective point," he ordered one general. "Wherever Lee goes, there you will go also."

★ McClellan was slow to attack and did so rarely, while Grant set assaults in motion on five different fronts at once, taking advantage of the Union's greater numbers. The most powerful was led by his friend and right hand, William Tecumseh Sherman, in Georgia.

The CSA's Robert E. Lee, outnumbered two to one, shrewdly dug in, trying to cause enough Union casualties that Northern voters would lose heart and press for peace. You felt the strain: in February 1864, you told a friend, "This war is eating my life out. I have a strong impression that I shall not live to see the end."

Grant made little headway in Virginia that spring but lost tens of thousands of men, partly because Lee's troops fought from trenches to defend every inch. Grant, understanding Lee's game, sent you a message: "There will be no turning back." You told John Hay any other commander would have retreated, but "it is the dogged pertinacity of Grant that wins."

FRONTLINE FATALITIES

YOU VISITED THE FRONT AND witnessed the awful suffering there. Your bodyguard will recall your sadness, "as indescribable as it was deep . . . I witnessed his agony when the thunder of cannon told him that men were being cut down like grass . . . I saw the anguish on his face when he came within sight of the poor, torn bodies of the dead and dying."

Over Mary's fierce and tearful opposition, you let your son Robert enlist and serve in Grant's HQ. You'd lost two boys to sickness already—why risk losing another to war? But Robert did not want to look like a coward, and you were getting ripped for sending only *other* people's sons into danger. In any case, Grant took care to keep Robert far from the actual fighting, so he came through without a scratch.

Your cabinet. Before you took office, someone warned you that your strong-willed cabinet members would eat you up. You answered that they would be just as likely to eat one another up. And so it has gone. You manage your cabinet masterfully, partly by taking advantage of their internal rivalries and partly because they all respect you enough to stay loyal.

Except for Salmon Chase, who constantly tries to undermine you. He does a good job as Treasury secretary, but he often criticizes you privately (and sometimes publicly). He even tried to challenge you for 1864's Republican presidential nomination. The nerve! Nonetheless, you've ignored the others' complaints about him, saying that Chase's ambition was just making him work harder, which was good for the country. Your sharp political instincts paid off when he dropped out of the running early in 1864 and you got the nomination without opposition.

The War at Home

YOUR FAMILY. **MARY IS STILL** mourning the loss of your son Willie, and she has not given up her séances. The hidden "spirits" at these sessions have shown some nerve themselves, pulling one cabinet member's beard and pinching another's ears.

Not that Mary is likely to care about your cabinet's comfort: she still dislikes and distrusts it. "If I listened to you," you say once, "I should soon be without a cabinet." Elizabeth Keckley considers Mary a shrewd judge of character whose intuitions about people's sincerity is "more accurate than that of her husband."

Mary's life has not been made any easier by her divided family loyalties. She's had *seven* brothers (or half brothers, or brothers-in-law) fighting for the CSA. She wants them to lose, of course, but not actually, you know, get *killed*.

Mary invited her favorite half sister, Emilie Todd Helm, to stay at the White House after her husband died fighting for the rebels. Mary wanted to comfort her, but the visit did *not* go well. First Emilie's little daughter got into fights with Tad over who was really president (she insisted it was Jefferson Davis). Then General Sickles came to dinner (minus the leg he lost at Gettysburg) with a senator who told Emilie, not very tactfully, "We have whipped the rebels at Chattanooga, and I hear, madam, that the scoundrels ran like scared rabbits." Southern pride offended, she responded, "It was the example . . . that you set them at Bull Run."

Taking you aside, Sickles rashly said you shouldn't be allowing rebels in the White House. "My wife and I are in the habit of choosing our own guests," you answered frostily. "We do not need from our friends either advice or assistance in the matter." Still, Emilie no longer felt comfortable in DC and left soon after.

With all this stress at home, it's amazing you still make jokes—though for you the stress requires them. Here are a few gems:

★ To John Hay: "The Lord prefers common-looking people; that is the reason He makes so many of them."

★ To a photographer who asks you to "just look

natural": "That is what I would like to avoid."

★ To a man requesting a pass to Richmond, the CSA capital: "Well, I would be very happy to oblige you, if my passes were respected; but the fact is, sir, I have, within the past two years, given passes to 250,000 men to go to Richmond, and not one has got there yet."

CLASH OF THE COPPERHEADS

DEMOCRATS. **THE MINORITY PARTY HAS** jumped on every unpopular decision the war has forced you to make, especially the national military draft you instituted in March 1863. The big problem: to satisfy pacifists, the draft let men avoid service by hiring substitutes or paying a three-hundred-dollar fee, and people who couldn't afford either way out hated the policy. Antiwar Democrats began calling the conflict a "rich man's war and a poor man's fight." In the terrible New York City draft riots of July 1863, poor whites (mostly immigrants) took their fury at the draft's unfairness out on innocent black people, killing more than a hundred. Thanks to the Emancipation

Proclamation, the rioters believed the Democratic party line that this war was really just about helping black slaves.

In August, you published a response to this argument: "You say you will not fight to free negroes. Some of them seem willing to fight for you; but, no matter. Fight you, then, exclusively to save the Union. I issued the proclamation on purpose to aid you in saving the Union."

But many Democrats have continued agitating against the war. Republicans call the protesters Copperheads, after the poisonous snake. Antiwar Dems have adopted the name as a badge of honor (literally), clipping pennies to show only the Goddess of Liberty's head and sticking the copper heads on their lapels. (Ironically, *your* head will appear on pennies starting in 1909, the first time any president receives that honor on a US coin.)

THE COPPERHEAD PARTY.—IN FAVOR OF A VIGOROUS PROSECUTION OF PEACE!

You found Clement Vallandigham, a congressman from Ohio, a particularly dangerous Copperhead. In a long January 1863 speech, he demanded that you quit trying to beat the CSA, saying war was getting the country nowhere. "Defeat, debt, taxation, sepulchers, these are your trophies. . . . I see more of barbarism and sin, a thousand times, in the continuance of this war . . . and the enslavement of the white race by debt and taxes and arbitrary power" than in black slavery. His influence provoked desertions, assaults on recruiting officers, and murders of free blacks.

In May you exiled Vallandigham to where you thought he belonged: the South. But the "apostle of peace," as his admirers called him, made his way to Canada, from which he continued to launch attacks on you and the war. You used the suspension of habeas corpus to arrest similar troublemakers, with this justification: "Must I shoot a simple-minded soldier boy who deserts, while I must not touch a hair of a wily agitator who induces him to desert? . . . I think that in such a case, to silence the agitator, and save the boy, is not only constitutional, but . . . a great mercy."

DOWN BUT NOT OUT

THE WAR (AND YOUR POPULARITY) reached a low point when one of Lee's generals invaded Maryland, getting within five miles of the White House.

Looking over a parapet, you were nearly hit by a CSA sniper. A young officer had to shout, "Get down, you damn fool, before you get shot."

To the American public, things looked grim. Even some Republicans questioned whether you were the right president to win this hard war. Not one but two of your (many) ex-generals came forward to challenge you for the presidency: McClellan for the Democrats and Frémont for a new party of radical abolitionists. Your chances for reelection looked slim; in August you told a visitor, "I am going to be beaten, and unless some great change takes place *badly* beaten."

The Democrats accused you of wanting full racial equality, even to the (then shocking) point of intermarriage. Calling themselves the white man's party, they even invented a new word for the "mixing of races" they claimed you were plotting—*miscegenation.* One Dem paper wrote that "tens of thousands of white men must bite the dust to allay the negro mania of the President." (Some Dem papers were subsidized by CSA agents based in Canada.)

Mary once again worked to get you elected, calling in favors to win you endorsements. She had many reasons, including one she confided only to her seamstress: "There is more at stake in this election than he dreams of. If he is reelected, I can keep him in ignorance of my [spending], but if he is defeated . . . he will know all." Despite Mary's flaws, you still adore her. You told a guest around that time, "My wife is as handsome as when she was a girl and I, a poor nobody then, fell in love with her, and [what's] more, have never fallen out."

Though you knew it might cost you the election, you did not try to change Grant's strategy of continuous attack. Far from it! You told him, "Hold on with a bull-dog grip, and chew & choke, as much as possible." Receiving this message, Grant laughed and told an aide, "The President has more nerve than any of his advisors."

SUCCESS IN THE SOUTH

ON SEPTEMBER 3, 1864, YOUR determination was finally rewarded. General Sherman wired, "Atlanta is ours, and fairly won." The tide of war had turned.

As the Union kept racking up victories, Frémont

withdrew from the presidential race, and you beat McClellan handily—BTW, with an even greater share of the soldiers' votes than of civilians'. Partly *because* the war was at such a critical stage (and suddenly going better), voters bought your campaign pitch that it is "not best to swap horses when crossing streams."

COSTLY CONSEQUENCES

EVEN BEFORE YOUR reelection, some Democrats hated you enough to threaten your life. One evening someone shot at you in the road, leaving a bullet hole in your stovepipe hat. Still, you refused the security measures

DIDYA KNOW?

Union soldiers weren't the only ones burning Atlanta. Just before losing the city, the Confederates put matches to munitions and supplies to keep them out of the Union's hands. General John Hood and his troops destroyed a supply train, causing a blast that damaged or demolished every building within a quarter mile, likely the biggest explosion of the entire war.

your bodyguard, Ward Lamon, recommended: "It would never do for a President to have guards with drawn sabers at his door, as if he fancied he were . . . an emperor."

Once your enemies realized they were facing four more years of Lincoln, the death threats multiplied. In December, Lamon was so upset by your lax approach to security that he wrote a scolding note: "I regret that you do not appreciate what I have repeatedly said to you in regard to . . . your household and your own personal safety. . . . You know, or ought to know, that your life is sought after, and will be taken unless you and your friends are cautious; for you have many enemies within our lines. . . . *You are in danger.*" Lamon even made you promise not to attend the theater, one of your favorite pastimes, if he was out of town—a promise you will not keep.

Even Republicans! Everyone's a critic. The abolitionists in your own party thought you moved way too slowly, while the conservative wing viewed you as a closet radical. (You must be doing something right to have annoyed so many people!) You staked out *your* position in November 1863, when you gave a speech dedicating the new military cemetery at Gettysburg.

A Man of Few Words

HISTORY WILL CALL IT THE Gettysburg Address, perhaps the greatest speech in US (if not world) history. You weren't the main speaker: Edward Everett, the former president of Harvard, gave the two-hour (!) principal oration. You were invited as an afterthought, to give "a few appropriate remarks." And did you ever!

LITTLE KNOWN FACTS ABOUT
THE GETTYSBURG ADDRESS:

1. While most modern presidents rely on the luxury of speechwriters, Abraham penned the entire (ahem, four-minute) address on his own.
2. The speech was only ten sentences long.
3. Only one photo of the president delivering the address exists, because it was so short. By the time photographers got their cameras set up, the speech was over! Only eighteen-year-old David Bachrach was able to snag a shot.

Your speech was over almost before people realized you'd begun it, but it said everything about why the war matters.

You reminded the country that America was "dedicated to the proposition that all men are created equal." That requires a "new birth of freedom," an America without slavery. But that's not all: America's foundation in human equality also makes it wonderfully unique. (Where else has democracy truly taken root? Russia? China? France? In 1863, they're all ruled by emperors. Even England still has a queen and allows only about one out of fourteen adults to vote.) This war must be won not only to free the enslaved, but so that "government of the people, by the people, for the people, shall not perish from the earth."

Not such a bad speech after all, Abe.

WARD HILL LAMON

People were so stunned by your powerful words that they did not applaud at first. Lamon will recall that you turned to him and said, "Lamon, that speech won't *scour*! It is a flat failure, and the people are disappointed." You have seldom been more wrong. Everett, by contrast, got it right in his gracious congratulatory letter: "I should be glad, if I could flatter myself that I came as near to the central idea of the occasion, in two hours, as you did in two minutes." (Of course, nothing could please the Democratic papers, one of which wrote, "The cheek of every American must tingle with shame as he reads the silly, flat, and dishwatery utterances. . . ." Biased much?)

Triumph for the Thirteenth Amendment

YOU ALSO BEGAN A SLOW, steady drive to make emancipation permanent. In April 1864, you wrote to a Kentucky newspaper, "I am naturally anti-slavery. If slavery is not wrong, nothing is wrong. I cannot remember when I did not so think, and feel." In a Baltimore speech two weeks later, you used a new metaphor to show why emancipation was right: "The shepherd drives the wolf from the sheep's throat, for which the sheep thanks the shepherd as a *liberator*, while the wolf denounces him for the same act as the destroyer of liberty, especially as the sheep was a black one."

In September 1864, you endorsed the idea of amending the Constitution to abolish slavery. Once reelected in November, you began pushing hard for it. You strengthened your case by pointing to the impact of black soldiers on the war effort. Although bigots had predicted they'd run from gunfire, black recruits had proven themselves to be brave fighters.

Vote by vote, you used all the many sticks and carrots at your disposal to get the necessary two-thirds majority in each house of Congress. Congressmen who voted with you were rewarded with goodies (such as federal jobs) for themselves and their families. When the Thirteenth Amendment finally won approval, in January 1865, one senator said ruefully, "The greatest measure of the nineteenth century was passed by corruption, aided and abetted by the purest man in America."

Technically, slavery will not be abolished until the end of 1865, when three-quarters of all states have ratified the amendment. But at the moment of passage in the House of Representatives, the gallery there exploded in cheers. Frederick Douglass read about it in a letter from his son, a Union soldier who was there to see it: "I wish you could have been here, such rejoicing I have never before witnessed (white people I mean)."

In 1820, Thomas Jefferson (the Declaration of Independence's main author *and* a Virginia slaveholder) wrote about America's awful dependence on slavery, in language you yourself once quoted: "We have the wolf by the ears, and we can neither hold him, nor safely let him go. Justice is in one scale, and self-preservation in the other." Decades later, Abraham, you have finally succeeded where the Founding Fathers failed: in freeing America from that bloody-jawed wolf once and for all.

THE CHOICE

THE WAR HAS ENTERED ITS final phase.

Sherman left Atlanta in ashes. "War is cruelty and you cannot refine it," he explained to the mayor, who perhaps disagreed. From there he cut a fifty-mile-wide swath of destruction through Georgia toward the Atlantic, meaning to damage the enemy's supply lines (farms, railroads), communication lines (telegraph wires), and especially morale. He instructed his men not to kill civilians but to destroy any property that could support the CSA's economy and its war effort.

On December 6, 1864, you said about Sherman, "We

all know where he went in at, but I can't tell where he will come out at." Within weeks he supplied the answer in this cable: "I beg to present you as a Christmas gift the City of Savannah with 150 heavy guns & plenty of ammunition & also about 25,000 bales of cotton." Since then, Sherman has been carving his way up through South Carolina, birthplace of the rebellion, to attack Lee from the rear.

General Grant himself is preparing a spring assault on Lee's last major stronghold. The war is almost won, but to your mind every soldier killed or wounded between now and then (on *both* sides) is an American. Do you keep fighting to the bitter end, or do you save lives by negotiating a truce? And if you do keep fighting, what will you do, once you've won, with the Confederate troops—and with the politicians and generals who led them and the civilians who supported them?

WHAT DO YOU DO, ABRAHAM? SELECT ONE:

A. Negotiate a truce.

You've already taken steps in this direction. Last month,

you met with CSA envoys to hash out details, but at that point the CSA's leadership wouldn't agree to rejoin the Union and accept emancipation.

Last December, your annual message to Congress predicted that Davis would not voluntarily dissolve the CSA: "Between him and us the issue is distinct, simple, and inflexible. It is an issue which can only be tried by war, and decided by victory."

So could you negotiate a truce if you wanted to?

B. Fight on, but show mercy to the rebels once you win.

Compassion has always been the core of your character, from the animals you wouldn't hunt to the deserters you pardon whenever possible. You also realize that *lasting* peace will be much harder if you impose harsh penalties on the defeated. You want victory to bring the country together, not drive it further apart.

As far back as December 1863, you issued a Proclamation of Amnesty and Reconstruction, allowing any state to reenter the Union if merely *10 percent* of its voters took a federal loyalty oath. Those voters who took the oath would escape penalty (unless they were high CSA officials) and could elect a new state government (that accepted emancipation). To furious abolitionists who complained that the proclamation was too lenient, you explained that it was meant to shorten the war.

But is there such a thing as too much mercy? As the abolitionists point out, the rebels have done everything in their power to perpetuate slavery and tear the country apart. Should they all get off scot-free?

C. Fight on, and punish the rebel leaders.

Once you win, it could make sense to spare the CSA rank and file. They may have fought against you, but the leaders bear most of the responsibility.

You're a generous person by nature, even to enemies closer to home. Salmon Chase, who betrayed you as Treasury secretary by bad-mouthing you to Congress and Republican leaders, who *still* thinks he's better than you— what did you do with him after accepting his (third) offer of resignation? You gave him a *promotion*. You named him in December to the dream job of chief justice of the Supreme Court, succeeding your late adversary Roger Taney. Your explanation: you and Chase "have stood together in the time of trial, and I should despise myself if I allowed personal differences to affect my judgment of his fitness for the office."

Sure, you had practical reasons. You knew Chase was likely to preserve your legacy if any of your antislavery acts came up before the court. Indeed, one of his first moves was to allow a black lawyer to argue cases before the court for the first time. By promoting Chase, you actually put him right where you wanted him. Your old friend Leonard Swett will recall that you were no naïve dummy: "He handled and moved men *remotely* as we do pieces upon a chessboard."

But you *also* have a rare immunity to grudges, a constant willingness to forgive for the greater good. Your mercy is such that even General Sherman admits he admired this quality in you: "Of all the men I have met, he seemed to possess more of the elements of greatness, combined with goodness, than any other."

D. Fight on, and punish all rebels.

You would certainly please many of your Northern supporters by showing that secession carries harsh penalties, for leaders and followers alike. The question is, will proving that point help or hurt the country as a whole over the longer run? If you want to discourage further discord, will punishment or clemency be more effective?

THE REVEAL

YOU CHOSE . . . B. **Fight on, but show mercy to the rebels once you win.** With the war nearly over, you deliver your second inaugural address, which history will proclaim as one of the greatest speeches ever given. Before a huge crowd, you call for understanding and forgiveness—for *both* sides. "Both read the same Bible, and pray to the same God; and each invokes His aid against the other. It may seem strange that any men should dare to ask a just God's assistance in wringing their bread from the sweat of other men's faces; but let us judge not, that we be not judged."

Perhaps slavery is an "offense" against God, you suggest, one for which the whole country shares historic blame—and for which God "gives to both North and South this terrible war" as punishment. In His wisdom, he may even make it "continue, until all the wealth piled by the [slaves'] two hundred and fifty years of unrequited toil shall be sunk, and until every drop of blood drawn with the lash, shall be paid by another drawn with the sword."

Let's win the war, you tell the country, not to punish the rebels but to end America's suffering: "With malice toward none; with charity for all; with firmness in the right, as God gives us to see the right, let us strive on to finish the work we are in; to bind up the nation's wounds; to care for him who shall have borne the battle, and for his widow, and his orphan—to do all which may achieve and cherish a just and a lasting peace among ourselves, and with all nations."

Way to set a high bar for future presidents, Abraham.

THE AFTERMATH

IN LATE MARCH, WITH LEE surrounded, you visit the front, where Grant asks how you want Davis and the other CSA leaders treated. You reply indirectly, with a joke about a man who's sworn off alcohol. When offered a choice of lemonade with or without whiskey, he says either is fine, provided no one *tells* him there's whiskey in it. Your clear hint: it may be just as well if the top rebels are allowed to "escape."

How come, when they've caused so much bloodshed? One reason is that you don't want the rebel leaders to become martyrs. Better they should slink off into exile than be put on public trial or, even worse, executed without trial. The country needs to move on from this awful conflict. As you later tell your cabinet, "Enough lives have been sacrificed. We must extinguish our resentments if we expect harmony and union."

But there's another reason. Your amazing empathy allows you to understand others' motives even when they do terrible things, and to see the best in them anyway. In that same cabinet meeting, you speak kindly of Lee and the other rebel generals, who you believe were just doing what they thought right.

Later you tell Grant that, after Lee surrenders, CSA soldiers should be allowed to go home. They have homes, families, jobs, maybe farms to tend, just as Union men do. You even recommend later that Grant leave them their guns to shoot crows with and their horses to plow with.

When Richmond, the Confederate capital, finally falls on April 2, you say, "Thank God I have lived to see this! It seems to me that I have been dreaming a horrid dream for four years, and now the nightmare is gone." You insist on touring the city ASAP despite possible danger, taking a moment to sit at Jefferson Davis's desk. Freed slaves recognize you and come running to shake your hand, bow to you, even kiss your boots, but you protest, "Don't kneel to me. That is not right. You must kneel to God only, and thank Him for the liberty you will enjoy hereafter."

On April 9, Lee finally surrenders to Grant at Appomattox Court House, Virginia. Grant lets him go. (In a fitting symbol, Lee's estate at Arlington, Virginia, has already been confiscated and turned into the country's largest military cemetery.) Grant feeds Lee's starving troops, telling his men, "The war is over, and the rebels are our countrymen again."

For you, they were always your countrymen. You never accepted the CSA's claims to be a *separate* country, and now you don't accept the radical Republicans' demands to treat it as a *conquered* country. The radicals claim that leaving the Union meant "state suicide" for every state that seceded, so now they should be demoted to mere "territories" (like New Mexico, say) under US control.

You disagree. You insist they remained states all along, just under the sway of rebels. In a victory celebration outside the White House on April 11, you tell the crowd that it's important to restore those states' "proper practical relation with the Union. . . . Finding themselves safely at home, it would be utterly immaterial whether they had ever been abroad." You even have the band play "Dixie," a favorite CSA song, saying it had always been one of your favorite tunes as well.

In your speech, you also propose giving voting rights to "very intelligent" blacks and those with army service. That enrages at least one person in the crowd: John Wilkes Booth, an actor who loves the South and whose hatred of you has been growing for years. In overdramatic style, he's been talking about doing something "heroic" to stop you, but it's this speech that pushes him over the edge. "This means [black] citizenship," he tells a friend. "Now, by God, I'll put him through. That is the last speech he'll ever make."

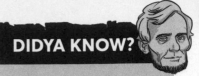

DIDYA KNOW?

Charles Colchester, a fake medium favored by Mary, warned Abe about a possible assassination. No magic required: Colchester was drinking buddies with John Wilkes Booth and probably overheard at least hints of Booth's evil plans.

"NOW HE BELONGS TO THE AGES"

ABOUT A WEEK BEFORE **B**OOTH uttered his fateful threat, you had a strange dream. You imagined you heard weeping in the White House and found a crowd in the East Room, sobbing around a corpse laid out on a bier. "Who is dead in the White House?" you asked a soldier who was standing guard. "The president," he answered. "He was killed by an assassin." Not a pleasant dream but all too true.

Your last full day of life was Good Friday, April 14. According to Elizabeth Keckley, your face that morning was "more cheerful than I had seen it in a long time."

You had a relaxed breakfast with your family, including your son Robert, your first opportunity to spend time with him since his return from war. You met with the cabinet, repeating your desire to see the rebel leaders treated leniently where possible.

You enjoyed a pleasant carriage ride with Mary in the afternoon. "Dear husband," she said, "you almost startle me by your great cheerfulness." You replied that you and Mary should "*both* be more cheerful in the future." You even started making plans for enjoying a quiet life together once you'd left office, perhaps traveling abroad. In the meantime, you were looking forward to the simple pleasure of attending a play, *Our American Cousin,* at Ford's Theatre that night.

LINCOLN'S BOX IN FORD'S THEATER

Booth, who had friends at most DC theaters, had learned of your plan for the evening. He saw an opportunity to become, as he imagined, a hero. Shockingly, he had little trouble entering the theater and slipping by your scant security. (Then again, no president had ever been assassinated.) As an experienced actor, Booth knew the play's most crowd-pleasing line; he timed his entry into your private box so that the audience's roar of enjoyment would keep your companions from hearing him. While you were still laughing, Booth aimed his gun, point-blank, at the back of your head—and fired.

The bullet, entering behind your left ear, immediately robbed you of consciousness. Booth drew a knife and stabbed one of your guests, then leapt from your box onto the stage and escaped out the back, soon to be hunted down and killed.

That was no use to you, though: you were beyond reviving. You were still breathing as men carried you to a modest boarding-house across the street, where they had to lay your long

DIDYA KNOW?

General Ulysses S. Grant was originally supposed to attend the play with Abe that fateful night. At the last minute Grant canceled. Later, he often said he wished he'd been there to help the president.

body diagonally across the normal-sized bed. People surrounded you all night long, trying to revive you, keeping guard, weeping quietly, or just standing in shock. Poor Mary, wailing and distraught, was eventually exiled to an adjoining room—a tragic omen of the miserable, wandering, lonely life she would lead for another seventeen years. When you died in the morning, it was Edwin Stanton, disdainful scoffer turned fervent admirer, who murmured, "Now he belongs to the ages."

You journeyed home to Illinois the same way you'd arrived for your inauguration: your body traveled

LINCOLN'S FUNERAL TRAIN

along the same train route back to Springfield, the town you so loved, where you were laid to rest. Stanton set a prolonged itinerary, with many stops over two weeks, which allowed the country to vent its anger at your cruel assassination. More than a million mourners came to pay their respects along the way, as the nation plunged into a grief that time has never quite cured.

During those two weeks, the people's extremely mixed perceptions of you changed, so that for most (including some in the South), you became a beloved martyr. Given your birth as the son of a carpenter and your murder on Good Friday, along with your mild disposition and moral courage, many even compared you to Jesus Christ. For black Americans who felt you had died for them, the blow fell especially hard. "No common mortal had died," wrote Elizabeth Keckley later, recalling another biblical hero to express her overwhelming grief. "The Moses of my people had fallen in the hour of triumph."

Sadly, the "hour of triumph" in the fullest sense had not yet arrived. General Lee had surrendered the largest part of the Confederate army, but others kept fighting even after Jefferson Davis was captured, on May 10. (To promote reconciliation, as you had urged, Davis was never tried for treason, instead being released after two years.) Even the Civil War's formal end in August did not completely end the fighting: resentful bands of Southern whites waged guerrilla, often terrorist warfare for decades against black citizens and federal law enforcement.

Maybe not even you, with your immense wisdom and political skills, could have succeeded in "binding up the nation's wounds" quickly after such a bitter conflict. Nevertheless, you would surely have done a better job of reconstruction in the South than your successor, Andrew Johnson, a Tennessee Democrat whose selection as your running mate in 1864 had helped you project a centrist image and get reelected. Johnson lacked both wisdom and skills, and his blatant Southern favoritism put him in constant conflict with the Republican-dominated Congress. Congress lurched in the opposite direction, imposing martial law on some states until 1877—after which it reversed, allowing horrendous "Jim Crow" laws to victimize Southern blacks socially, economically, and politically for nearly a century. Overall, America's leaders botched any chance of a just and peaceful transition after the war you won. Our nation still bears the scars of that failure.

So your death, Abraham, was a catastrophe not just for your family and fellow citizens but also for future generations. You of all people, though, would not have wanted us to dwell on your life's tragic ending. No, you would have wanted us instead to be thankful that you lived your life as you did, and for as long as you could. When America counts its blessings, Abraham, you must always be among them.

Once again, it all comes back to the choices you made. Another person would have chosen differently, and our world would have been the poorer for it. Your choices not only took you from nowhere (as it seemed) to the summits of national glory, but they also revealed the unique combination of qualities that *made* you Abraham Lincoln. In fact, our country can be proud of a political system that, however flawed, produced at our darkest hour a president with those very qualities.

What qualities? Well, here are six that helped determine your choices, making all the difference in your success—and the nation's. Perhaps not coincidentally, these qualities also represent much of what makes *America* so special; after all, our nation's culture shaped you, and you certainly shaped it. Because you were a complicated man, just as we're a complicated country, your crucial qualities each came with their own contra-dictions. You weren't perfect, not completely one thing or another—which actually makes you more American.

YOU WERE SELF-RELIANT. Your rough-hewn early life, which would allow you to campaign as the Rail-Splitter and a man of the people, could have destroyed a lesser person, but instead it tempered you. Growing up so poor bred your self-reliance; reading books so deeply (because you had so few) expanded your self-knowledge; losing your mother and sister so young increased your self-sufficiency; bearing your father's harsh treatment so resolutely developed your self-assurance; and overcoming your early business failures so honorably built your self-respect. Most politicians have more privileged upbringings, leaving them with less preparation for the demands of public life.

Yet your self-reliance was not absolute: you depended on allies' help and teamwork for nearly all your major accomplishments. Your self-knowledge was a work in progress: you were constantly searching your soul, questioning your own decisions, and writing agonized notes to yourself as you wrestled with important issues. Your self-sufficiency did not save you from periodic bouts of abysmal melancholy or stop you from needing

Mary's love and the companionship of your many friends. Your self-assurance did not lead to arrogance; you showed deep respect for others' opinions and God's power. And your self-respect did not mean you took yourself too seriously; you were always ready to laugh at yourself, the key to your amazing knack of making others laugh with you.

YOU WERE PRACTICAL. The hard realities of frontier life made you extremely pragmatic. As a lawyer, you were known for meticulous attention to detail and relevant cases. As a legislator, you favored commerce and infrastructure projects. As a candidate, you maintained a keen interest in the blocking and tackling necessary to a campaign. As president, you strove to remain within the legal and institutional limits of your power. As commander in chief, despite your lack of military experience, you succeeded by devoting yourself to tactical fine points and the use of new technologies.

Yet you were also a man in love with language and ideas. As a lawyer, you charmed juries with your jokes and impressed judges with your conceptual understanding. As a legislator, you were guided by party loyalty and even more by the philosophy for which your party stood. As a candidate, you appealed to voters' overarching ideals. As president, you inspired the nation with speeches that soared to the level of poetry. And as commander in chief, you kept in mind both your strategic vision and the larger goals for which you were fighting the war.

YOU WERE PRINCIPLED. Good old Honest Abe. You took great trouble to pay your debts. You kept your promises when possible. You won people's trust by telling the truth. Yet you were also very clever about avoiding questions, answering them on your own terms or turning them aside with funny stories. You could be downright devious in confusing a witness, overcoming an opponent, or cornering a cabinet secretary. And you did not hesitate to use all the means at your disposal, including horse trading and favor peddling, to win the passage of laws that mattered to you.

You lived according to principle—for instance, stepping aside for Lyman Trumbull in your first senatorial campaign in order to fight the spread of slavery. Yet one of your most powerful principles was moderation— even in the battle for principle itself. You frequently angered extremists on both sides of a question by trying to find a workable middle ground.

Slavery provides the clearest example. You believed

that one person should never be able to own another, and over time there's no doubt you earned your name of Great Emancipator. When you took office, though, it is unlikely you actually intended to free the slaves. Even at your inauguration, you expressly stated that you had "no lawful right" to uproot slavery in states where it already existed. If your generals had been better, or the Confederacy's worse, it's quite possible that the war would have ended before you felt the military need—and popular support—to take *any* action on emancipation. In retrospect, though, even Frederick Douglass saw the strategic upside in your hesitation:

HAD HE PUT THE ABOLITION OF SLAVERY BEFORE THE SALVATION OF THE UNION, HE WOULD HAVE INEVITABLY DRIVEN FROM HIM A POWERFUL CLASS OF THE AMERICAN PEOPLE AND RENDERED RESISTANCE TO THE REBELLION IMPOSSIBLE. VIEWED FROM THE GENUINE ABOLITION GROUND, MR. LINCOLN SEEMED TARDY, COLD, DULL, AND INDIFFERENT; BUT MEASURING HIM BY THE SENTIMENT OF HIS COUNTRY, A SENTIMENT HE WAS

BOUND AS A STATESMAN TO CONSULT,
HE WAS SWIFT, ZEALOUS, RADICAL, AND
DETERMINED.

YOU WERE GENEROUS. With your "original gorilla" face and ragged clothes, you started life at a social disadvantage. Your size, strength, humor, and character helped you win friends, but not before you developed a keen empathy for those even less fortunate. Your reluctance to hunt animals, your readiness to help others (such as the drunkard you rescued that night in Indiana), your gentleness with Mary and the boys, your willingness to put the disloyal Salmon Chase on the Supreme Court, your clemency to deserters and cowards, your merciful instincts toward the defeated rebels: all demonstrate a rare generosity of heart.

Yet your empathy was not always beneficial; for example, your boys could perhaps have used a bit more paternal discipline. Empathy did not stop you from waging battle; you are still the only president to spend virtually his entire time in office conducting a major war. And empathy, ironically, could often serve as a weapon; by putting yourself in others' places, you could anticipate their arguments and strategies. It turns out that empathy often helped you best your adversaries.

YOU WERE EGALITARIAN. Your empathy, together with your respect for others, strengthened your belief in the importance of human dignity. Just as America gave you opportunities that few men of humble birth could have enjoyed in other countries, so you felt that *all* Americans, black and white, should have the right to rise, the freedom to work and enjoy the fruits of their own labor. That was a major reason you offered for hating slavery.

Yet you stated clearly that the right to liberty did not mean the races were equal, or should be treated equally, in every way. As Frederick Douglass later admitted, "President Lincoln was a white man, and shared the prejudices common to his countrymen toward the colored race." Douglass, who understood you better than most, accepted that flaw in you as a necessary evil: "Looking back to his times and to the condition of his country, we are compelled to admit that this unfriendly feeling on his part may be safely set down as one element of his wonderful success in organizing the American people for the tremendous conflict before them, and bringing them safely through that conflict." By 1865 your views had evolved, so that you were ready to propose political equality for at least some blacks, but we will never know whether you would eventually have progressed all the way to full equality.

YOU WERE DEMOCRATIC. You believed passionately in the democratic principles on which America was founded. You developed uncanny skill both at understanding public opinion and at using your masterful PR to shift it. "Father Abraham" was many Northerners' affectionate nickname for you, and you secured it through word as well as deed. Why did you take such pains to keep the people's approval? Sure, you needed it to win reelection and to keep Congress and the states in line, but you also agreed with the Founding Fathers that any government's legitimacy must rest on the consent of the governed.

Yet a substantial minority of Northerners called you by a less affectionate name: Dictator. When you unilaterally suspended the constitutional right of habeas corpus in 1861, they said you trampled on sacred American liberties. When you played your war-powers card in order to mobilize troops and arrange your naval blockade, they called you a tyrant. When Congress backed you, they claimed you were exploiting the national emergency to launch one-man rule over the entire country. When the war dragged on, they even accused you of prolonging it to satisfy your own lust for power.

Now, these critics largely disagreed with your goals as president, not just your methods, so they were hardly unbiased. You thought seriously about each infringement, exercised restraint whenever you thought you could, and frequently reined in your generals as well. But your actions set perilous precedents, which some later administrations used to override civil liberties far more than you did. Here, as in so many other areas, your legacy is hardly simple or spotless.

Self-reliant. Practical. Principled. Generous. Egalitarian. Democratic. You were all these things, Abraham, but not only, or always, these things. More than most presidents, you faced high-stakes choices fraught with complexity. On the other hand, you yourself were about as complex as presidents come. Could it have been your own richly paradoxical nature that enabled you to navigate those crossroads with the subtlety they required?

However you accomplished it, Abraham, we can be thankful that you chose as you did.

HONEST ABE

ORIGINAL GORILLA

RAIL-SPLITTER

DICTATOR

THE GREAT EMANCIPATOR

FATHER ABRAHAM

A TIMELINE OF ABE'S LIFE

1809: Born near Hodgenville, Kentucky, on February 12 to Thomas Lincoln and Nancy Hanks Lincoln

1816: Family moved to Indiana

1818: Mother died of "milk sick"

1819: Father married the widow Sarah Bush Johnston

1828: Sister, Sarah, died in childbirth; Abe and a friend steered a flatboat of cargo to New Orleans

1830: Family moved to Illinois

1831: Abe settled in New Salem, Illinois; began working at Offutt's general store

1832: Ran for state assembly; served in Black Hawk War; Offutt's store closed, but Abe bought another store with partner William Berry

1833: Abe's store failed, leaving him deep in debt; became New Salem postmaster

1834: Won seat in state assembly; met Stephen Douglas

1835: William Berry died, increasing Abe's debt; Abe's sweetheart Ann Rutledge died

1836: Received license to practice law

1837: Moved to Springfield, Illinois; entered law partnership with John Stuart

1839: Met Mary Todd

1840: Became engaged to Mary

1841: Broke off engagement; entered law partnership with Stephen Logan

1842: Married Mary

1843: Son Robert (Bobbie) born

1844: Bought house in Springfield; started own law practice with William Herndon

1846: Son Edward (Eddie) born; Abe elected to Congress

1848: Challenged President Polk with speeches on Mexican War

1849: Received patent for boat flotation system

1850: Eddie died; son William (Willie) born

1851: Father died

1853: Son Thomas (Tad) born

1854: Took up politics again to combat Kansas-Nebraska Act

1855: Lost election for Senate to Lyman Trumbull

1856: Joined Republican Party

1858: Won murder acquittal for Duff Armstrong; ran for Senate against Stephen Douglas

1860: Delivered speech at Cooper Union; won presidential nomination at Republican Convention in Chicago; won presidency against three other candidates, including Stephen Douglas; Southern states began seceding

1861: Took office as president; sent relief expedition to Fort Sumter, which Confederacy attacked, launching Civil War; suspended habeas corpus in Maryland; Stephen Douglas died; put George McClellan in charge of Union army

1862: Son Willie died; announced Emancipation Proclamation

1863: Signed Emancipation Proclamation; delivered Gettysburg Address

1864: Appointed Ulysses S. Grant to command Union army; defeated McClellan to gain reelection

1865: Oversaw passage by Congress of the Thirteenth Amendment, ending American slavery; delivered second inaugural address; celebrated surrender of Confederate General Robert E. Lee; died April 15 after being shot by John Wilkes Booth

WHO'S WHO

Robert Anderson—major in the Union army; commander of Fort Sumter at the start of the Civil War

Duff Armstrong—son of Abe's New Salem friend Jack Armstrong; on trial for murder, acquitted with Abe's help

Jack Armstrong—leader of the Clary's Grove Boys in New Salem; challenged Abe to wrestling match; later became Abe's friend and supporter

Edward Baker—Illinois congressman and Abe's friend

Edward Bates—Missouri politician and contender for the 1860 Republican presidential nomination; joined Abe's cabinet as attorney general

Grace Bedell—New Yorker, age eleven, whose letter persuaded Abe to grow his beard

John Bell—Tennessee politician; 1860 presidential nominee of the Constitutional Union Party

William Berry—Abe's inept business partner in New Salem

Montgomery Blair—Maryland lawyer who represented Dred Scott before the Supreme Court; served as Abe's postmaster general

John Wilkes Booth—actor and Confederate sympathizer; decided that Abe was a tyrant who must die to avenge the South

John Breckinridge—Kentucky politician who served James Buchanan as vice president; 1860 presidential nominee of the Southern Democrats

John Brown—abolitionist who led violent raids in Kansas and Virginia; hanged after seizing the US armory in Harpers Ferry

James Buchanan—president before Abe; did little to help preserve the Union

Ambrose Burnside—failed Union general; grew massive whiskers that were later dubbed "sideburns" in his honor

Andrew Butler—South Carolina senator and promoter of the Kansas-Nebraska Act

Benjamin Butler—Massachusetts lawyer and Union general; established policy of "confiscating" slaves used by Confederate army

Simon Cameron—Pennsylvania politician and a contender for 1860 Republican presidential nomination; joined Abe's cabinet as secretary of war, but too incompetent to last long

Peter Cartwright—revivalist preacher; lost to Abe in 1846 Illinois congressional race

Salmon Chase—Ohio politician and contender for 1860 Republican presidential nomination; joined Abe's cabinet as Treasury secretary, but kept trying to undermine him; Abe accepted his resignation and later appointed him to Supreme Court

David Davis—Illinois judge and Abe's close friend

Jefferson Davis—president of the Confederate States of America

Stephen Douglas—accomplished Illinois Democrat; Abe's rival for Senate, the presidency, and Mary's affection

Frederick Douglass—abolitionist and former slave; praised Abe's measures against slavery, but often wished those efforts were stronger and sooner

Elizabeth Edwards—Mary's sister; looked down on Abe at first and advised Mary not to marry him

Jesse Fell—secretary of the Illinois Republican Committee; early supporter of Abe for president

Millard Fillmore—moderate Whig who succeeded Zachary Taylor as president in 1850; last president affiliated with neither Democrats nor Republicans

John C. Frémont—led US armed forces into California before Mexican War; served Union army as general; issued order (canceled by Abe) freeing slaves in Missouri; briefly opposed Abe in 1864 election

Ulysses S. Grant—chronic underachiever who proved himself in the Union army; put in command by Abe in early 1864; accepted Lee's surrender in Virginia

Horace Greeley—editor of the *New York Tribune;* supported Abe in 1860, but often criticized him later for being too slow to ban slavery and end the war

Sarah Lincoln Grigsby—Abe's beloved sister; died in childbirth when Abe was nineteen

Dennis Hanks—Abe's cousin on his mother's side; lived with the family during Abe's childhood

John Hardin—Illinois congressman; Mary's distant cousin

John Hay—Abe's secretary from 1860 on

Emilie Todd Helm—Mary's favorite half sister; stayed at the White House after her husband died fighting in the Confederate army

William Herndon—Abe's junior law partner; no fan of Mary

Joseph Hooker—overconfident Union general

Andrew Johnson—Democrat from Tennessee who succeeded Abe as president; not up to the job

Norman Judd—Chicago politician and friend of Abe; cost Abe a Senate seat in 1855, but helped him win the Republican presidential nomination in 1860

Elizabeth Keckley—Mary's seamstress and confidante; born a slave

Ward Lamon—Illinois lawyer; friend and bodyguard of Abe

Robert E. Lee—primary leader of Confederate army; previously captured John Brown at Harpers Ferry

Edward (Eddie) Lincoln—Abe's second son; died at age three

Mary Todd Lincoln—Abe's wife; born to wealth in Kentucky; saw potential in Abe that few others perceived

Nancy Hanks Lincoln—Abe's mother; died when he was nine

Robert (Bobbie) Lincoln—Abe's oldest son; served in Union army under Grant

Sarah Bush Johnston Lincoln—Abe's beloved stepmother

Thomas Lincoln—Abe's father; rugged frontier carpenter and farmer; tough dad to get along with

Thomas (Tad) Lincoln—Abe's youngest son; bedeviled

White House staff and visitors; died at the age of eighteen

William (Willie) Lincoln—Abe's third son; died in the White House at age eleven

Stephen Logan—senior partner at Abe's second law firm; later advised him during 1855 Senate campaign

Joel Matteson—Illinois governor who ran as a Democrat in 1855 Senate campaign

George McClellan—Union general who often found reasons not to attack; ran as a Democrat in 1864 presidential election, with no more success

Irvin McDowell—Union general who lost the Civil War's first major battle

George Meade—Union general who won the Battle of Gettysburg, but then let Lee and his army escape to safety

John Nicolay—Abe's second secretary, joining John Hay

Denton Offutt—storekeeper who gave Abe his first job in New Salem

Mary Owens—Abe's first fiancée; the romance fizzled

Franklin Pierce—Democratic president who backed Kansas-Nebraska Act

Allan Pinkerton—private detective who warned of a

plot to kill Abe on his way to the inauguration; later gathered intelligence for the Union army

James Polk—Democratic president during the Mexican War, which Abe opposed

Ann Rutledge—Abe's first real romance; died of typhoid in 1835

Dred Scott—slave whose claim to freedom was rejected by the Supreme Court's inflammatory decision; eventually freed by new owners

Winfield Scott—Abe's first military leader in the Civil War; too old and ill for the job

William Seward—Abe's secretary of state; previously New York governor and senator; Abe's top rival for the 1860 Republican presidential nomination

James Shields—Illinois Democrat; Abe's dueling opponent; later senator

Daniel Sickles—New York politician, acquitted of murder on the grounds of temporary insanity; "political general" whose insubordination at Gettysburg cost many lives and his own leg

Caleb Smith—Abe's first secretary of the interior

Joshua Speed—Abe's roommate in Springfield; lifelong friend

Edwin Stanton—Abe's secretary of war; accomplished

Pennsylvania lawyer who had little respect for Abe before actually working for him

John Todd Stuart—senior partner of Abe's first law firm; cousin of Mary; Illinois congressman

Charles Sumner—abolitionist senator from Massachusetts

Leonard Swett—Illinois lawyer and close friend of Abe

Roger Taney—chief justice of the Supreme Court; decided against Dred Scott; tried to stop Abe from suspending habeas corpus

Zachary Taylor—Whig president for whom Abe campaigned; died after a year in the White House

Julia Jayne Trumbull—Mary's close friend, until her husband defeated Abe in the 1855 Senate election

Lyman Trumbull—Abe's rival for Senate in 1855; as senator, pushed Abe to attack the seceded states

Clement Vallandigham—Ohio antiwar Democrat who often criticized Abe, both before and after Abe exiled him to the Confederacy

Gideon Welles—Abe's secretary of the navy

ABE'S HISTORIC FIRSTS

You grew up on the American frontier, Abe, so it's no wonder that as president you were a true trailblazer. Not only did you abolish slavery and lead the country to victory in the Civil War, but you achieved an impressive list of other historic firsts, big and small:

- First president with a beard
- First president who did not previously serve as vice president, secretary of state, senator, or general
- First Republican president
- First president not born in one of the original thirteen colonies/states
- First president whose wife was called "First Lady"
- First president to appear on a US coin
- First (and only) president with a US patent
- First president photographed at inauguration
- First president to institute a federal income tax

- First president to declare a national holiday of Thanksgiving
- First president to "pardon" a turkey at Thanksgiving
- First and only president to connect the east and west coasts via transcontinental railroad (launched by you, completed after your death)
- First president to make effective use of the telegraph
- First president to be assassinated

Oh, and here's one little-known way in which you were not first but last: the last president who agreed to fight a duel. Luckily, you and your opponent, James Shields, managed to work things out before blood was shed. If only the North and the South could have done the same!

ABE THE JOKESTER

For a melancholy man, Abe, you sure knew how to be funny. The chapters above describe some of your famous jokes and pranks, but there were plenty more where those came from. A few:

- You once complimented a man as being the first fellow you knew who wore Sunday clothes during the week.

- When you heard that Mary's family had changed their name from Tod, you said one "d" was good enough for God, but not for the Todds.

- When you were in Congress, someone wrote asking you for "a signature with a sentiment," to which you replied, "I am not a very sentimental man, and the best sentiment I can think of is, that if you collect the signatures of all persons who are no less distinguished than I, you will have a very undistinguishing mass of names."

- You liked to joke that you were "the long of it," while Mary was "the short of it." She did not share your amusement, and in fact would not be photographed standing with you.

- In court, you told a joke about a sailor whose ship was about to sink. The sailor was not a religious man, but he was desperate. He cried out that God knew how seldom he prayed, but if God would help him just this once, he promised it would be a long time before he bothered God again.

- You loved Springfield, but occasionally you dissed it in jest. You told a story about a minister who came to preach about "the second coming of the Lord." A city resident told him not to bother, because "if the Lord's seen Springfield once, He ain't coming back."

- In 1856, you told a potentially hostile audience that you were like the ugly horseman who went out riding one day. A woman complained, "Well, for land sake, you are the homeliest man I ever saw." The horseman said, "Yes, madam, but I can't help it," to which the woman replied, "No, I suppose not, but you might stay at home."

- Running against Stephen Douglas for the Senate, you called one of his arguments "as thin as the homeopathic soup that was made by boiling the shadow of a pigeon that had starved to death."

- During your last debate with Douglas, you noted that Douglas was feuding with the head of his own Democratic Party. You declared you were like the old lady who saw her husband fighting a bear. Not sure who was going to win, she decided to hedge her bets, yelling, "Go it, husband! Go it, bear!"

- On your way to Washington in 1861, you would tell crowds you had come to see them and let them see you, in which you had "the best of the bargain."

- Speaking to a group of newspaper editors, you joked that you were like a man attacked by a robber looking for money, who said, "My dear fellow, I have no money, but if you will go with me to the light, I will give you my note [IOU]."

- When you saw an opera diva's large, flat feet, you commented, "The beetles wouldn't have much of a chance there."

- As president, you were constantly pestered by people asking for special favors, which you were often not able to grant. When you came down with varioloid, a mild form of smallpox, you joked, "Now I have something I can give everybody."

- John Hay wrote in his diary, "The President said the Army dwindled on the march like a shovelful of fleas pitched from one place to the other."

- You once said you knew a man so short that when he walked through the snow, the seat of his pants wiped out his own footprints.

- Before showing your cabinet a draft of the Emancipation Proclamation, you read them a few funny stories. When they grew impatient, you said, "Gentlemen, why don't you laugh? With the fearful strain that is upon me night and day, if I did not laugh I should die, and you need this medicine as much as I do."

- Your friends, who distrusted Salmon Chase and his presidential ambitions, advised you to remove him from the Treasury Department long before you did. You explained that Chase was like a plow horse, and his ambition was biting him like a horsefly—but at least the fly made the horse keep going. Why get rid of Chase and his horsefly, so long as they kept the department going?

- One of your favorite jokes, which you loved to retell, was actually made by your son Tad on Election Day, 1864. You asked Tad if his pet turkey would be voting, to which Tad cleverly answered, "He is underage."

- When you decided to accept Louisiana's post-occupation government despite its flaws, believing it would evolve into something better: "We shall sooner have the fowl by hatching the egg than by smashing it."

ABE THE WRITER

Abe, you had less than a year of schooling in your whole life, but you read enough on your own to make up for it. Many historians believe you were the best writer ever to live in the White House. Here are a few examples of your most famous passages:

- From speech on the Kansas-Nebraska Act, 10/16/1854:

  > The Missouri Compromise ought to be restored. For the sake of the Union, it ought to be restored. We ought to elect a House of Representatives which will vote its restoration. If by any means, we omit to do this, what follows? Slavery may or may not be established in Nebraska. But whether it be or not, we shall have repudiated—discarded from the councils of the Nation—the SPIRIT OF COMPROMISE; for who after this

will ever trust in a national compromise? The spirit of mutual concession—that spirit which first gave us the constitution, and which has thrice saved the Union—we shall have strangled and cast from us forever. And what shall we have in lieu of it? The South flushed with triumph and tempted to excesses; the North, betrayed, as they believe, brooding on wrong and burning for revenge. One side will provoke; the other resent. The one will taunt, the other defy; one aggresses, the other retaliates.

· From the seventh Lincoln-Douglas debate, 10/15/1858:

[Slavery] is the real issue. That is the issue that will continue in this country when these poor tongues of Judge Douglas and myself shall be silent. It is the eternal struggle between two principles—right and wrong—throughout the world. They are the two principles that have stood face to face from the beginning of time; and will ever continue to struggle. The one is the common right of humanity and the other the divine right of kings. It is the same principle in whatever shape it develops itself. It is the same spirit that says, "You work and toil and earn bread, and I'll eat it." No matter in what shape it comes, whether from the mouth of a king who seeks to bestride the people of his own nation and live by the fruit of their labor, or from one race of men as an apology for enslaving another race, it is the same tyrannical principle.

- From a speech in New Haven, Connecticut, 3/6/1860:

If I saw a venomous snake crawling in the road, any man would say I might seize the nearest stick and kill it; but if I found that snake in bed with my children, that would be another question. I might hurt the children more than the snake, and it might bite them. . . . But if there was a bed newly made up, to which the children were to be taken, and it was proposed to take a batch of young snakes and put them there with them, I take it no man would say there was any question how I ought to decide! That is just the case! The new Territories are the newly made bed to which our children are to go, and it lies with the nation to say whether they shall have snakes [i.e., slavery] mixed up with them or not. It does not seem as if there could be much hesitation what our policy should be!

- From the First Inaugural Address, 3/4/1861:

  [Speaking to the Southern states] In *your* hands, my dissatisfied fellow countrymen, and not in *mine,* is the momentous issue of civil war. The government will not assail *you.* You can have no conflict, without being yourselves the aggressors. *You* have no oath registered in Heaven to destroy the government, while *I* shall have the most solemn one to "preserve, protect and defend" it.

- From a special message to Congress, 7/4/1861:

  This is essentially a People's contest. On the side of the Union, it is a struggle for maintaining in the world, that form and substance of government, whose leading object is, to elevate the condition of men—to lift artificial weights from all shoulders . . . to afford all an unfettered start, and a fair chance, in the race of life.

• From the Annual Message to Congress, 12/1/1862:

[On emancipation] The dogmas of the quiet past are inadequate to the stormy present. The occasion is piled high with difficulty, and we must rise with the occasion. As our case is new, so we must think anew, and act anew . . . Fellow citizens, *we* cannot escape history. We of this Congress and this administration will be remembered in spite of ourselves. . . . The fiery trial through which we pass will light us down, in honor or dishonor, to the latest generation. We *say* we are for the Union. The world will not forget that we say this. We know how to save the Union. The world knows we do know how to save it. We—even *we here*—hold the power, and bear the responsibility. In *giving* freedom to the *slave,* we *assure* freedom to the *free*— honorable alike in what we give, and what we preserve. We shall nobly save, or meanly lose, the last best hope of earth. Other means may succeed; this could not fail. The way is plain, peaceful, generous, just—a way which, if followed, the world will forever applaud, and God must forever bless.

· Address at Gettysburg, Pennsylvania, 11/19/1863: Four score and seven years ago our fathers brought forth on this continent a new nation, conceived in Liberty, and dedicated to the proposition that all men are created equal.

Now we are engaged in a great civil war, testing whether that nation, or any nation so conceived and so dedicated, can long endure. We are met on a great battlefield of that war. We have come to dedicate a portion of that field, as a final resting place for those who here gave their lives that

that nation might live. It is altogether fitting and proper that we should do this.

But, in a larger sense, we cannot dedicate—we cannot consecrate—we cannot hallow—this ground. The brave men, living and dead, who struggled here, have consecrated it, far above our poor power to add or detract. The world will little note, nor long remember, what we say here, but it will never forget what they did here. It is for us the living, rather, to be dedicated here to the unfinished work which they who fought here have thus far so nobly advanced. It is rather for us to be here dedicated to the great task remaining before us—that from these honored dead we take increased devotion to that cause for which they gave the last full measure of devotion—that we here highly resolve that these dead shall not have died in vain—that this nation, under God, shall have a new birth of freedom—and that government of the people, by the people, for the people, shall not perish from the earth.

- From speech to the 166th Ohio Regiment, 8/22/1864:

    It is not merely for today, but for all time to come that we should perpetuate for our children's children this great and free government, which we have enjoyed all our lives. I beg you to remember this, not merely for my sake, but for yours. I happen temporarily to occupy this big White House. I am a living witness that any one of your children may look to come here as my father's child has. . . . It is for this the struggle should be maintained, that we may not lose our birthright. . . . The nation is worth fighting for, to secure such an inestimable jewel.

- Letter to Mrs. Lydia Bixby, 11/21/1864:

    Dear Madam, I have been shown in the files of the War Department . . . that you are the mother of five sons who have died gloriously on the field of battle. I feel how weak and fruitless must be any words of mine which should attempt to beguile you from the grief of a loss so overwhelming. But I cannot refrain from tendering to you the consolation that may be found in the thanks of the Republic they died to save. I pray that our Heavenly Father may assuage the anguish of your bereavement, and leave you only the cherished memory of the loved and lost, and the solemn pride that must be yours, to have laid so costly a sacrifice upon the altar of Freedom. Yours, very sincerely and respectfully,

Abraham Lincoln

WHAT WOULD ABE THINK?

Abe, you passed away a century and a half ago. The world has changed a lot since then! We've seen things you might never have even imagined. From what you did and said, though, we can guess what you might have thought of them. Here's a random selection, ordered roughly by timing:

Communism—Karl Marx, father of communism, actually sent you a fan letter in late 1864, congratulating you on being reelected and praising you for freeing the slaves. You did not share his view, however, that most things should be owned by "the people" (i.e., government) and not by individual people. You never voiced big doubts about capitalism, you represented big companies as a lawyer, and you would have hated the Soviet and Chinese dictatorships that arose in communism's name.

Airplanes—You piloted a flatboat all the way

to New Orleans, you filed a patent to prevent riverboats from getting stuck on shoals, you focused your law practice on railroads, and you pushed for completion of the transcontinental railroad. As a major supporter of better transportation, you would have marveled at mankind's new ability to fly coast to coast in a few hours. Toward the end of your life, you told Mary you were looking forward to traveling to Europe and maybe even the Holy Land once your term ended. How cool would it have been to *fly* there?

Antibiotics—You'd have given anything for these. If only your first love (Ann Rutledge) and your son Willie had survived typhoid fever! Antibiotics could have saved them, as well as the countless Civil War soldiers who perished from battlefield infections.

Nuclear weapons—You were never warlike, despite overseeing America's biggest war ever. So doomsday weapons would not have appealed to you. On the other hand, you might have cheered when the atom bomb ended World War II. You knew all too well that war can produce horrific casualties when the losing side insists on dragging it out. You might also have credited nuclear arms with helping to prevent another world war since then.

Pizza—Meh. You never paid much attention to food, often being content at meals with an apple, a piece of bread, and a glass of water. You would have liked seeing your kids enjoy pizza, but it probably wouldn't have made a huge difference in your own life.

Man on the moon—Wow! You would have been awed by this triumph of human ingenuity. You would also have been delighted to see a united America, launching from a Southern state, reach the moon first. A bit of astronomy, of course, helped you win your most famous murder case, when you used an almanac to prove there could not have been enough moonlight for the witness against Duff Armstrong to see him commit the crime.

Microwave ovens—You would have welcomed the convenience of these handy devices, particularly since you never cared so much about the quality of what you ate. Anything that saved Mary trouble, of course, would have been okay by you.

Factory farms—Your dad worked you hard in the field, so you had little sentimental attachment to the idea of the small family farm. You wouldn't have opposed consolidation that created bigger spreads and allowed investment in new technologies. One of your law clients, in fact, made mechanical reapers. By creating the land-grant universities and the US Department of Agriculture, you also promoted the spread of farming know-how. The main problem you might have had with "agribusiness": because you loved animals of all kinds, you would have pressed for more humane treatment of creatures such as pigs and chickens.

Video games—You were an "early adopter" of home entertainment technology, buying a stereopticon ("magic lantern" for viewing photo slides) for your home in Springfield. You and your boys would surely have spent happy hours playing the early video games, such as Space Invaders, Asteroids, and Donkey Kong.

Karaoke—You loved hearing your friends

perform, such as bodyguard Ward Lamon playing the banjo and singing. But you couldn't carry a tune yourself, so you seldom sang, at least in public.

The Internet—All the world's knowledge available at your fingertips? What's not to like, especially for a self-educated man? You also spent whatever time you could reading newspapers, even from the Democrats and Southerners. Think how efficiently you could have tracked public opinion by surfing the Web.

Reality TV—You loved stories and getting insights into the lives of other people. Reality TV stars are not exactly ordinary folks, but the shows focusing on other lifestyles and regions would definitely have gotten your attention.

Business casual—As a man who barely noticed clothes and went barefoot whenever possible, you would have welcomed this trend with open (short-sleeved) arms.

Genetic engineering—Genetic medicine would have impressed you as a potential boon for public health, but you might have been wary of "designer genes" that mess with nature. You had great respect for divine power and the role that fate plays in all our lives.

Music streaming—Even early in your career, you took many opportunities to attend shows and concerts. You would have leapt at the chance to carry music wherever you went.

Netflix—You loved theater, which offered one of your favorite means of relaxation as president, so TV and movies would have delighted you.

Texting—You were ahead of your time, using telegrams the way people today use email. You set up a telegraph office in the War Department, next door to the White House, and on many days spent hours there communicating with generals in the field. You would have taken to texting right away.

Emoji—You were always seeking new ways to connect with people. You used all the means at your command to communicate with them on an emotional level, whether in speeches, in letters, or face to face. Your likely response to emoji: ☺

Climate change—As a fan of transportation,

technology, and corporations, you would probably not be at the forefront in fighting climate change. On the other hand, you did care about conservation, signing a bill to protect the Yosemite Valley in 1864, an action that set a precedent for our national park system.

An African American president—You became more open-minded about black people over the course of the war. You spoke in favor of granting at least some blacks the vote, which marked you as ahead of your time. In 1865, you might have had a hard time wrapping your mind around the idea of a black president; on the other hand, if you had somehow lived until now, your views would have continued to evolve. You would probably have applauded the election of a black president in 2008—even if he *was* a Democrat.

A potential woman president—You were a man of your epoch, and so did not naturally view women as political equals to men. You never spoke out for women's voting, though you mentioned it in passing in one 1836 letter. You did take Mary's political advice seriously, but you would probably have scratched your head at the idea of a "lady president." Of course, if you had somehow lived another 150 years, you would probably have changed with the times, since you were already ahead of your own.

RECOMMENDED READING

ABRAHAM LINCOLN

Abraham Lincoln Presidential Library Foundation. *Under Lincoln's Hat: 100 Objects That Tell the Story of His Life and Legacy.* Lanham: Lyons Press, 2016.

Freedman, Russell. *Abraham Lincoln & Frederick Douglass: The Story Behind an American Friendship.* New York: Clarion Books, 2012.

Giblin, James Cross. *Good Brother, Bad Brother: The Story of Edwin Booth & John Wilkes Booth.* Boston: Clarion, 2005.

Giovanni, Nikki. *Lincoln and Douglass: An American Friendship.* New York: Square Fish, 2013.

Herbert, Janis. *Abraham Lincoln for Kids: His Life and Times with 21 Activities.* Chicago: Chicago Review Press, 2007.

Judson, Clara Ingram. *Abraham Lincoln: Friend of the People.* London: Young Voyageur, 2016.

Lincoln, Abraham. *Lincoln's Gettysburg Address.* Park Ridge: Albert Whitman & Company, 2013.

McComb, Marianne. *The Emancipation Proclamation.* Washington, DC: National Geographic, 2006.

McPherson, James M. *Abraham Lincoln.* Oxford: Oxford University Press, 2009.

Wheeler, Tom. *Mr. Lincoln's T-Mails: The Untold Story of How Abraham Lincoln Used the Telegraph to Win the Civil War.* New York: HarperBusiness, 2006.

THE CIVIL WAR

Armstrong, Jennifer. *Photo by Brady: A Picture of the Civil War.* New York: Atheneum, 2005.

DK Eyewitness Books: Civil War. New York: DK Children, 2015.

Murphy, Jim. *The Boys' War: Confederate and Union Soldiers Talk About the Civil War.* Boston: Houghton Mifflin, 1993.

Murphy, Jim. *The Long Road to Gettysburg.* Boston: Sandpiper, 2008.

Sheinkin, Steve. *Two Miserable Presidents: The Amazing, Terrible, and Totally True Story of the Civil War.* New York: Square Fish, 2009.

Thompson, Ben. *Guts & Glory: The American Civil War.* New York: Little, Brown Books for Young Readers, 2015.

Vonne, Mira. *Gross Facts About the U.S. Civil War.* North Mankato, MN: Capstone Press, 2017.

WEBSITES OF INTEREST

Abraham Lincoln Online, abrahamlincolnonline.org

Abraham Lincoln Papers at the Library of Congress,
memory.loc.gov/ammem/alhtml/malhome.html

Abraham Lincoln's Classroom, abrahamlincolnsclassroom.org

The Civil War, civilwar.com

The Collected Works of Abraham Lincoln, quod.lib
.umich.edu/l/lincoln

50 Interesting Facts About Abraham Lincoln's Life,
blog.constitutioncenter.org/2014/02/50-shades-of
-abraham-lincoln-2

The History Place Lincoln Timeline, historyplace.com
/lincoln

A Lincoln Library, alincoln-library.com

The Lincoln Log, thelincolnlog.org

The Miller Center at the University of Virginia,
millercenter.org/president/lincoln

Mr. Lincoln & Friends, mrlincolnandfriends.org

This Day in the Civil War, civilworg/150th-anniversary
/this-day-in-the-civil-war.html

WHERE TO "VISIT" ABE TODAY

SPRINGFIELD, ILLINOIS

Abraham Lincoln Presidential Library and Museum, illinois.gov/alplm/Pages/default.aspx

Lincoln Home National Historic Site, nps.gov/liho/index.htm

Lincoln Law Office, illinois.gov/ihpa/Experience/Sites/Central/Pages/Lincoln-Herndon.aspx

Lincoln Tomb State Historic Site, illinois.gov/ihpa/Experience/Sites/Central/Pages/Lincoln-Tomb.aspx

Old State Capitol State Historic Site, illinois.gov/ihpa/Experience/Sites/Central/Pages/Old-Capitol.aspx

ELSEWHERE

Abraham Lincoln Birthplace National Historic Park, Hodgenville, KY, nps.gov/abli/index.htm

Cooper Union, New York, NY, cooper.edu/about/history/foundation-building-great-hall

Ford's Theatre National Historic Site, Washington, DC, nps.gov/foth/index.htm

Gettysburg National Military Park, Gettysburg, PA, nps.gov/gett/index.htm

Lincoln Boyhood National Memorial, Lincoln City, IN, nps.gov/libo/index.htm

Lincoln Log Cabin State Historic Site, Lerna, IL, lincolnlogcabin.org

Lincoln Memorial, Washington, DC, nps.gov/linc/index.htm

Lincoln's New Salem State Historic Site, Petersburg, IL, lincolnsnewsalem.com

President Lincoln's Cottage at the Soldiers' Home, Washington, DC, lincolncottage.org

IMAGE CREDITS

Library of Congress

1, 2, 8, 17, 32, 33, 35, 36, 38, 42, 44, 54, 55, 62, 63, 66, 80, 81, 89, 97, 121, 125, 139 (both), 142, 146, 147, 183, 186, 188, 199, 203, 204, 214, 221, 232, 236, 238

Wikipedia Commons

6, 23, 39, 40, 65, 71, 74, 76, 78, 83, 87, 98, 100, 102, 116, 118, 122, 140, 150, 163, 170, 176, 181

Flickr Commons

4, 9, 46, 179 (both), 205

iStock

91, 157

A NOTE FROM THE AUTHORS

This first book in our biography series takes place during one of the most troubling crises in our country's history—the civil war—and yet Abraham Lincoln, for all his struggles, may have been our funniest president ever. So we have to wonder, do dangerous times call for leaders with a sense of humor? Maybe humor is one way to achieve the perspective that people need if they're going to make wise decisions.

Decisions, you see, are the real stars of this series. *Crisis* is the ancient Greek word for "turning point"; Abe earned his place in history by deciding *which way* to turn. He made mistakes along the way, but who doesn't? His missteps are interesting in themselves and show that our amazing president was still a human being. And, of course, ordinary people (including kids) who have their own choices to make can learn from Abe's good *and* bad decisions.

Writing about Abe was an incredible experience. We started by reading up on him a bit, then chose ten of his key life decisions for closer focus. It wasn't easy settling on just ten: the man had no shortage of important choices to make! Then we dove into the books, hit the Web, and planned our trip to Springfield, Illinois. Abe spent most of his adult life there, and it was in Springfield that we really began to understand what a complicated person he was. Behind the icon was a real human being, in whose home, law office, and statehouse office we gained new perspective on what it was like being Abe. A big shout-out, also, to Springfield's Abraham Lincoln Presidential Library and Museum, which has done a fantastic job of presenting the Rail-Splitter in the context of his bewildering, dramatic times.

Once back from Springfield, we started writing. Each of us picked choices to write about, and then we edited each other's work, sending chapters back and forth until we thought the manuscript was ready for our wonderful editor, Phoebe Yeh. *She* found lots of ways to improve it, so it was back to our laptops—and that was before the talented copy editors, art directors, and other pros had their say. It's been a challenging but exhilarating process, and we can't think of anyone we'd rather have inspiring and informing it than the Man in the Stovepipe Hat. He really was an exceptional person.

We hope you enjoy reading this book as much as we enjoyed writing it together!

LEILA AND TOM HIRSCHFELD

TOM HIRSCHFELD is a *New York Times* bestselling author whose books include *Business Dad: How Good Businessmen Can Make Great Fathers (and Vice Versa)*. His daughter **LEILA HIRSCHFELD** is a Harvard College history major. When they're not writing biographies together, they like to travel, play Scrabble, and take turns feeding Flash the Wonder Frog.